"Your golden will always love you for yourself. Your wealth or social or professional success are not important to it. It gives its love unquestionably and completely; what greater devotion can anyone demand?"
Jamie J. Sucher, Golden Retrievers, *1987*

Love of
Goldens

Todd R. Berger, Editor

Photography by Alan and Sandy Carey

Foreword by Roger Caras

Voyageur Press

PetLife
LIBRARY

Compiled and edited by Todd R. Berger
Designed by Kristy Tucker
Printed in Hong Kong

99   00   01   02   5   4   3

Library of Congress Cataloging-in-Publication Data

Love of goldens / Todd R. Berger, editor ; photography by Alan and Sandy Carey ; foreword by Roger Caras.
    ISBN 0-89658-385-6
    1. Dogs—Fiction. 2. Golden retriever—Fiction. 3. Human-animal relationships—Fiction. 4. Short stories, American.
    5. Short stories, English. I. Berger, Todd R., 1968- . II. Series.
    PS648.D64L6 1998
    813' .01083629772—dc21   98-17603
                          CIP

Published by Voyageur Press, Inc.
123 North Second Street, P.O. Box 338, Stillwater, MN 55082 U.S.A.
651-430-2210, fax 651-430-2211

Page 1: *Redefining the word "cute," a golden puppy pauses for just a second during a romp across the backyard.*
Page 2–3: *A majestic golden in a winter wonderland.*
Page 3: *A Christmas pup snoozes amidst the colorful toys and packages of the holiday season.*
Page 6: *The gentle temperament of golden retrievers endears them to children—of all ages.*

Above: *A golden retriever bonds well with its boy and will remain forever faithful by his side—particularly when there's a potential after-dinner snack involved.*

Contents

Foreword 9

by Roger Caras

Introduction 13

The Most Wonderful Dog in the World 21

"A Mind of Its Own" 23

by Dean Koontz

"My Reluctant Retriever" 43

by David Morine

Golden Days 53

"Sports Afield with a Golden Receiver" 55

by Timothy Foote

"Lily's Gift" 67

by Karyn Kay Zweifel

"Early Bird Memories" 95

by Todd Tanner

A Place in Our Hearts 103

"Broken Treaty" 105

by Dion Henderson

"Mrs. Donovan" 129

by James Herriot

Foreword

by Roger Caras

 Over the span of fifteen thousand years (at least!) since man began extracting the domestic dog from the loins of a small subspecies of wolf an incredible number of things have happened. Very early in the process, although we can assume that early man knew nothing whatever of genetics, the process of selection began. Wolf/dogs with desirable or even endearing characteristics were allowed to breed, or at least the easy keepers among them were kept alive, and so they did breed.

The results of that process are bewildering in their variety today. The American Kennel Club has a list of 153 breeds and varieties that they recognize plus a roster of eight to ten under the heading *Miscellaneous Breeds* for whom recognition will come in the next few years. But worldwide the list of distinct breeds numbers somewhere between 450 and 850! If we add to that bewildering number the breeds that became extinct over the past millennia, the parade is truly amazing.

Now consider just one breed, the golden retriever. A litter of four puppies resulting from the cross of a flat-coated retriever with the now-extinct Tweed spaniel in the last half of the nineteenth century went on to leave their pawprints across the pages of our history of the dog. There is no breed more admired than their descendants, the dearly beloved golden. There are many wonderful companion breeds, of course, and aesthetics, interest in utility, and personal experience establish individual favorites, but on virtually every list of favorites compiled in the last hundred years, the golden is there.

". . . the most golden part about a golden retriever is his heart."—Roger Caras

The reasons for the incredible popularity of the golden are not difficult to discern. The golden is beautiful, a wonderful, solid dog with a face that seems to smile without loss of dignity. The golden is intelligent, one of the most intelligent of all breeds. He takes to training as easily as he does to water. He accepts responsibility as demonstrated by the number of his kind that are assigned to lead the blind and perform other assistance tasks for handicapped owners. The golden is not petty or quarrelsome and gets on well with both cats and other dogs as well as livestock. Above all, the golden naturally bonds with adults and children of our species. He has a huge heart and he readily shares it with anyone willing to bond with him. The golden is generous and outgoing, endlessly affectionate and loyal. In fact, the most golden part of a golden retriever is his heart. He is everything we could possibly want a dog to be whether he is in the field as a gun dog or in the home as a child's companion. If you doubt any of this, read on and see what expressions of wonder and love have come from the real-life experiences of some of the world's most articulate dog lovers.

Roger Caras is the President of the American Society for the Prevention of Cruelty to Animals and the author of seventy books on animals and the environment.

Golden retrievers—especially puppies—love to give just about anything a good chew. Add some competition, and this natural tendency becomes an integral part of a playful battle over a throw hoop.

Introduction

The golden retriever is the most wonderful dog in the world. It is beautiful, smart, and unflappably nice. With a talent for everything from Frisbee catching to duck retrieving, a golden retriever takes its place as an integral member of the family from day one. That piddling pup with the button nose and floppy ears snuggles up close, and even when grown and chasing a car, a squirrel, or a tennis ball, you can still feel the warmth at your side. After a short time, it becomes impossible to remember what life was like before that reddish-haired, shaggy beast came into your home. The golden quickly finds its way into your heart.

And you're not alone. Some 70,000 golden retrievers are registered with the American Kennel Club (AKC), 7,500 in Canada, and 15,000 in the United Kingdom. Used for everything from waterfowling in the North American flyways to sniffing for survivors after the Oklahoma City bombing to therapy dogs in a Liverpool home for the elderly, the golden is at home almost anywhere.

But it is as the ultimate family dog that the golden has risen to prominence. With the temperament of a teddy bear and looks as stunning as the latest Hollywood starlet, what's not to like? This is one dog that you won't have to worry about around the kids, that will get your newspaper for you, that is incredibly easy to train. Sure, she eats a lot, knocks stuff off the coffeetable with her tail, and gets an infinite number of burrs caught in her fur after a jaunt in the woods. No dog is perfect, but the golden, arguably, comes closest.

". . . the golden is proof that beauty and brains can go together."—Kurt Unkelbach, The American Dog Book, *1976*

Loved by everyone from former U.S. President Gerald Ford to the Maharajah of Junagadh, India, and immortalized by Buddy the basketball-playing golden retriever in the movie *Air Bud*, the golden has legions of fans. But, surprisingly, in the history of humans and dogs, the golden is very much the new kid on the block.

A golden retriever quickly finds its way into your heart—and lap.

A Brief History of the Golden

Like so many dog breeds developed for retrieving, the golden traces its origins to nineteenth-century Great Britain. Prior to the development of the retriever breeds, British hunters primarily used pointers, setters, and water spaniels to retrieve game. The Labrador retriever has earlier origins than the golden, but by the mid-1800s, some breeders began to ponder the possibility of developing a yellow retriever.

Until 1952, the origin of the golden retriever was a colorful mystery, as unsubstantiated rumors prevailed that Sir Dudley Marjoribanks of Guisachan, Inverness-shire, Scotland—the first Lord Tweedmouth, if you prefer—purchased six or eight Russian circus dogs from a traveling big top in Brighton and that these dogs were the founders of today's golden retriever breed. A strange story, to say the least, given that there is no evidence that Lord Tweedmouth ever had any sort of Russian circus dog in his kennel. Nonetheless, this was the assumed origin of the breed until about fifty years ago.

But in 1952, the sixth Earl of Ilchester, the great-nephew of the first Lord Tweedmouth, sent tremors through the golden retriever world when he published his research of his great-uncle's kennel stud book. The meticulous records documented all dogs in Lord Tweedmouth's kennels between 1835 and 1890, and there is no mention of any Russian dogs. The true origin of the golden retriever could finally be known.

In 1865, Lord Tweedmouth purchased his first yellow retriever, which he described as a "sport," or abnormality, in a litter of blacks. This yellow retriever, named Nous, appears in photographs from the era as a larger golden with a wavy coat. In 1868, Lord Tweedmouth bred this retriever with a Tweed water-spaniel named Belle. The Tweed water-spaniel is now extinct, but is believed to be a strain of the Irish water-spaniel with a light, liver-colored coat and close curls. The mating of Nous and Belle resulted in four yellow puppies, and these tiny fluffballs formed the foundation of today's golden retriever. Lord Tweedmouth bred subsequent generations with flat- and wavy-coated retrievers, red setters, and bloodhounds. By 1913, the British Kennel Club accepted the golden, or yellow, retriever as a distinct breed, settling on the designation "retriever (golden)" in 1920.

The first golden retrievers probably were imported into North America in 1881. At that time, the Hon. Archie Marjoribanks, son of Lord Tweedmouth, brought two goldens with him to his ranch in Texas. Ishbel Marjoribanks, a daughter of Lord Tweedmouth and the wife of the Governor General of Canada, is pictured with a golden in a photo taken in 1894 in Ottawa. But despite these upper-crust dogs on North American soil, it took several decades for the breed to catch on.

The first golden retriever kennel in North America was founded at Winnipeg in 1918. The American Kennel Club registered its first golden in 1925, followed by registration with the Canadian Kennel Club in 1927. Speedwell Pluto, an imported golden who was described by breeder Ralph Boalt of Winona, Minnesota, as "big, powerful, handsome, and courageous," brought attention to the breed by winning an American bench championship in 1933, followed by a Canadian championship. This dog was the "foundation sire" for the breed in the United States. The first National Retriever Field Trial champion, a golden called King Midas of Woodend, solidified the breed's reputation by winning his title in 1941. The golden would go on to win many more titles.

These golden pups look like little butterballs as they hang up their legs in a neighborhood swingset.

The popularity of the golden in North America surged. In 1932, twenty goldens were registered with the AKC. By 1964, that number had risen to nearly 4,000, soaring further to today's 70,000. The golden retriever has risen to the title of "the ultimate family dog" not because it could take on the other retriever breeds on a national stage, but because its "need-to-please" temperament and gentle nature made it a congenial member of the household. As Joan Tudor

Unlike humans, the golden retriever has the ability to make it rain with a good shake seemingly involving every muscle of its spasmodic body.

put it in her book *The Golden Retriever*, "The usefulness of goldens as gundogs, their beauty and their excellence as companions quickly became recognised," and the golden retriever was here to stay.

About *Love of Goldens*
Love of Goldens is the first book of its kind, collecting stories and photographs of the golden child of the dog world. There are so many facets to the character of the golden, and *Love of Goldens* touches on many. You will read the writing of the legendary James Herriot, who penned a story of a golden retriever who never loses his faith in humankind despite monstrous cruelty. You will read David Morine's story of Percy, his squirrel-chasing, birdfeeder-guarding golden, and "Sports Afield with a Golden Receiver" by Timothy Foote, which delves into the intricacies of tennis-ball

Sweet Partings

by David Kliman

My golden retriever, Casey Indiana Jones, has always been the perfect, most gorgeous, queen of the countryside. Saved from the pound 11 years ago, to this day she is the love of my dog life. She always has a smile on her face and has never done much wrong until just recently. I was leaving for Europe on business and two nights before a very early morning departure, I took my passport in its fine Italian leather case and placed it on my desk. Not thinking much about it, I went out to dinner. Upon returning home, I found Casey hiding in a bathroom and my passport case and its contents shredded on the dining room floor.

"My golden retriever, Casey Indiana Jones, has always been the perfect, most gorgeous, queen of the countryside."

Luckily, the U.S. Passport office was open the next morning, and I was able to secure an emergency replacement in just a few hours.

I surmised that doggie instincts might be better than my own and wondered if intercontinental travel was indeed wise. But logic prevailed and I reckoned that Miss Jones, reared on rawhide, simply found the aroma of fine leather too good to pass up. The passport was really incidental.

But showing up at the passport office with my mutilated document in a zip lock bag with that "Sorry Officer, the dog ate my homework" look on my face must have been a sight to be seen.

Karma? The trip was a huge success. Downside? I lost 4 years worth of really cool visas and entry stamps—memories—gone but not forgotten.

It made me feel good to know that my girl Casey would try almost any trick in the book to keep me at home!

David Kliman is a vice president of a California insurance company and a lifetime dog lover.

football with a canine wide receiver. John J. Kelley describes his running partner Brutus, and Todd Tanner tells the tale of a certain golden retriever and a certain man who both lived for the hunt. Dean Koontz contributes an excerpt from his thriller *Watchers*, and Karyn Kay Zweifel haunts the psyche, in a good way, with a story of ghostly puppies.

Alan and Sandy Carey contribute their best work to illustrate *Love of Goldens*. The Careys have spent years photographing golden retrievers to create a body of work unrivaled in the photographic world. This is the finest collection of golden retriever images ever assembled.

The underlying theme is love and admiration for the golden retriever—the most wonderful dog in the world.

The owner of this mucky pack of goldens was smart not to use his Buick with the leather interior for this trip afield.

The golden retriever is an athlete, with a vigorous body and a smooth, powerful gait.

PART I

The Most Wonderful Dog in the World

"Surely if God could look like something of this world that we could all see and relate to, it would more than likely be a Golden Retriever."
Debra Marlin, Yellowdog, 1997

Above: *A golden sprints across the shallows of a Rocky Mountain lake.*
Left: *A typically reddish golden retriever strikes a pose on a sun-shiny December day.*

A Mind
of Its Own

by Dean Koontz

 To say that a golden retriever has a kind heart is to state the obvious. The temperament of this wonderful dog is renowned, and there is nothing more satisfying to a golden then to please his master. And even with strangers, goldens will quickly learn to trust, even if the world they grew up in was less than kind.

Dean Koontz is a suspense writer of the highest order. His tension-filled stories seem to inhabit the chest of the reader, as the muscles anxiously tighten while the fates of his characters unfold.

Many of his numerous books feature dogs, including *Dragon Tears, Dark Rivers of the Heart, Ticktock,* and *Fear Nothing.* As Koontz wrote, "Through the character of a dog, I can say things about the human condition that are simple and true yet palatable, even if sometimes harsh, because the dog's perception is colored by an endearing innocence."

Watchers was Koontz's first book to feature a canine main character, Einstein, a golden retriever of unusual intelligence. The book is not only the story of a man and his dog, but a thriller and a love story as well, and the book is considered one of Koontz's greatest. This excerpt comes from early in *Watchers,* as the main (human) character, Travis, starts to realize there's something unusual about the dissheveled golden retriever he found in the woods.

❧

Kind in temperament and loyal to its master until death do they part, the golden retriever is the most wonderful dog in the world.

AT MCDONALD'S ON East Chapman Avenue in Orange, Travis Cornell had ordered five hamburgers for the golden retriever. Sitting on the front seat of the pickup, the dog had eaten all of the meat and two buns, and it had wanted to express its gratitude by licking his face.

"You've got the breath of a dyspeptic alligator," he protested, holding the animal back.

The return trip to Santa Barbara took three and a half hours because the highways were much busier than they had been that morning. Throughout the journey, Travis glanced at his companion and spoke to it, anticipating a display of the unnerving intelligence it had shown earlier. His expectations were unfulfilled. The retriever behaved like any dog on a long trip. Once in a while, it *did* sit very erect, looking through the windshield or side window at the scenery with what seemed an unusual degree of interest and attention. But most of the time it curled up and slept on the seat, snuffling in its dreams—or it panted and yawned and looked bored.

When the odor of the dog's filthy coat became intolerable, Travis rolled down the windows for ventilation, and the retriever stuck its head out in the wind. With its ears blown back, hair streaming, it grinned the foolish and charmingly witless grin of all dogs who had ever ridden shotgun in such a fashion.

In Santa Barbara, Travis stopped at a shopping center, where he bought several cans of Alpo, a box of Milk-Bone dog biscuits, heavy plastic dishes for pet food and water, a galvanized tin washtub, a bottle of pet shampoo with a flea-and-tick-killing compound, a brush to comb out the animal's tangled coat, a collar, and a leash.

As Travis loaded those items into the back of the pickup, the dog watched him through the rear window of the cab, its damp nose pressed to the glass.

Getting behind the wheel, he said, "You're filthy, and you stink. You're not going to be a lot of trouble about taking a bath, are you?"

The dog yawned.

By the time Travis pulled into the driveway of his four-room rented bungalow on the northern edge of Santa Barbara and switched off the pickup's engine, he was beginning to wonder if the pooch's actions that morning had really been as amazing as he remembered.

"If you don't show me the right stuff again soon," he told the dog as he slipped his key into the front door of the house, "I'm going to have to assume that I stripped a gear out there in the woods, that I'm just nuts and that I imagined everything."

Standing beside him on the stoop, the dog looked up quizzically.

"Do you want to be responsible for giving me doubts about my own sanity? Hmmmmm?"

An orange and black butterfly swooped past the retriever's face,

startling it. The dog barked once and raced after the fluttering prey, off the stoop, down the walkway. Dashing back and forth across the lawn, leaping high, snapping at the air, repeatedly missing its bright quarry, it nearly collided with the diamond-patterned trunk of a big Canary Island date palm, then narrowly avoided knocking itself unconscious in a head-on encounter with a concrete birdbath, and at last crashed clumsily into a bed of New Guinea impatiens over which the butterfly soared to safety. The retriever rolled once, scrambled to its feet, and lunged out of the flowers.

When it realized that it had been foiled, the dog returned to Travis. It gave him a sheepish look.

"Some wonder dog," he said. "Good grief."

He opened the door, and the retriever slipped in ahead of him. It padded off immediately to explore these new rooms.

"You better be housebroken," Travis shouted after it.

He carried the galvanized washtub and the plastic bag full of

With such cute puppy-dog eyes, this golden youngster hardly looks like it would make a spirited stand to defend its precious rope toy.

Right: *The golden retriever was developed for hunting, and most goldens are quite at home on an autumn day in the field. However, the golden's normally luxuriant coat will collect enough burrs, stick-tights, and other pieces of debris to keep its owner busy for hours after the hunt is over.*

Below: *Three golden retrievers sitting on the edge of a snow-covered forest. Golden retrievers not only get along well with humans of all shapes and sizes, they rarely quarrel with other members of their own species.*

other purchases into the kitchen. He left the food and pet dishes there, and took everything else outside through the back door. He put the bag on the concrete patio and set the tub beside it, near a coiled hose that was attached to an outdoor faucet.

Inside again, he removed a bucket from beneath the kitchen sink, filled it with the hottest water he could draw, carried it outside, and emptied it into the tub. When Travis had made four trips with the hot water, the retriever appeared and began to explore the backyard. By the time Travis filled the tub more than half full, the dog had begun to urinate every few feet along the whitewashed concrete-block wall that defined the property line marking its territory.

"When you finish killing the grass," Travis said, "you'd better be in the mood for a bath. You reek."

The retriever turned toward him and cocked its head and appeared to listen when he spoke. But it did not look like one of those smart dogs in the movies. It did not look as if it understood him. It just looked dumb. As soon as he stopped talking, it hurried a few steps farther along the wall and peed again.

Watching the dog relieve itself, Travis felt an urge of his own. He went inside to the bathroom, then changed into an older pair of jeans and a T-shirt for the sloppy job ahead.

When Travis came outside again, the retriever was standing beside the steaming washtub, the hose in its teeth. Somehow, it had managed to turn the faucet. Water gushed out of the hose, into the tub.

For a dog, successfully manipulating a water faucet would be very difficult if not impossible. Travis figured that an equivalent test of his own ingenuity and dexterity would be trying to open a child-proof safety cap on an aspirin bottle with one hand behind his back.

Astonished, he said, "Water's too hot for you?"

The retriever dropped the hose, letting water pour across the patio, and stepped almost daintily into the tub. It sat and looked at him, as if to say, *Let's get on with it, you dink.*

He went to the tub and squatted beside it. "Show me how you can turn off the water."

The dog looked at him stupidly.

"Show me," Travis said.

The dog snorted and shifted its position in the warm water.

"If you could turn it on, you can turn it off. How did you do it? With your teeth? Had to be with your teeth. Couldn't do it with a paw, for God's sake. But that twisting motion would be tricky. You could've broken a tooth on the cast-iron handle."

The dog leaned slightly out of the tub, just far enough to bite at the neck of the bag that held the shampoo.

"You won't turn off the faucet?" Travis asked.

Whatever it takes to keep cool on a steamy summer day.

The dog just blinked at him, inscrutable.

He sighed and turned off the water. "All right. Okay. Be a wiseass." He took the brush and shampoo out of the bag and held them toward the retriever. "Here. You probably don't even need me. You can scrub yourself, I'm sure."

The dog issued a long, drawn-out *woooooof* that started deep in its throat, and Travis had the feeling it was calling *him* a wiseass.

Careful now, he told himself. You're in danger of leaping off the deep end, Travis. This is a damn smart dog you've got here, but he

can't really understand what you're saying, and he can't talk back.

The retriever submitted to its bath without protest, enjoying itself. After ordering the dog out of the tub and rinsing off the shampoo, Travis spent an hour brushing its damp coat. He pulled out burrs, bits of weeds that hadn't flushed away, un-snarled the tangles. The dog never grew impatient, and by six o'clock it was transformed.

Groomed, it was a handsome animal. Its coat was predominantly medium gold with feathering of a lighter shade on the backs of its legs, on its belly and buttocks, and on the underside of the tail. The undercoat was thick and soft to provide warmth and repel water. The outer coat was also soft but not as thick, and in some places these longer hairs were wavy. The tail had a slight upward curve, giving the retriever a happy, jaunty look, which was emphasized by its tendency to wag continuously.

The dried blood on the ear was from a small tear already healing. The blood on the paws resulted not from serious injury but from a lot of running over difficult ground. Travis did nothing except pour boric-acid solution, a mild antiseptic, on these minor wounds. He was confident that the dog would experience only slight discomfort—or maybe none at all, for it was not limping—and that it would be completely well in a few days.

The retriever looked splendid now, but Travis was damp, sweaty, and stank of dog shampoo. He was eager to shower and change. He had also worked up an appetite.

The only task remaining was to collar the dog. But when he attempted to buckle the new collar in place, the retriever growled softly and backstepped out of his reach.

"Whoa now. It's only a collar, boy."

The dog stared at the loop of red leather in Travis's hand and continued to growl.

"You had a bad experience with a collar, huh?"

The dog stopped growling, but it did not take a step toward him.

"Mistreated?" Travis asked. "That must be it. Maybe they choked you with a collar, twisted it and choked you, or maybe they put you on a short chain. Something like that?"

The retriever barked once, padded across the patio, and stood in the farthest corner, looking at the collar from a distance.

"Do you trust me?" Travis asked, remaining on his knees in an unthreatening posture.

The dog shifted its attention from the loop of leather to Travis, meeting his eyes.

"I will never mistreat you," he said solemnly, feeling not at all foolish for speaking so directly and sincerely to a mere dog. "You must know that I won't. I mean, you have good instincts about things like that, don't you? Rely on your instincts, boy, and trust me."

The dog returned from the far end of the patio and stopped just beyond Travis's reach. It glanced once at the collar, then fixed him with that uncannily intense gaze. As before, he felt a degree of communion with the animal that was as profound as it was eerie— and as eerie as it was indescribable.

He said, "Listen, there'll be times I'll want to take you places where you'll need a leash. Which has to be attached to a collar, doesn't it? That's the only reason I want you to wear a collar—so I can take you everywhere with me. That and to ward off fleas. But if you really don't want to submit to it, I won't force you."

For a long time they faced each other as the retriever mulled over the situation. Travis continued to hold the collar out as if it represented a gift rather than a demand, and the dog continued to stare into his new master's eyes. At last, the retriever shook itself, sneezed once, and slowly came forward.

"That's a good boy," Travis said encouragingly.

When it reached him, the dog settled on its belly, then rolled onto its back with all four legs in the air, making itself vulnerable. It gave him a look that was full of love, trust, and a little fear.

Crazily, Travis felt a lump form in his throat and was aware of hot tears scalding the corners of his eyes. He swallowed hard and blinked back the tears and told himself he was being a sentimental dope. But he knew why the dog's considered submission affected him so strongly. For the first time in three years, Travis Cornell felt needed, felt a deep connection with another living creature. For the first time in three years, he had a reason to live.

He slipped the collar in place, buckled it, gently scratched and rubbed the retriever's exposed belly.

"Got to have a name for you," he said.

The dog scrambled to its feet, faced him, and pricked its ears as if waiting to hear what it would be called.

God in heaven, Travis thought, I'm attributing human intentions to him. He's a mutt, special maybe but still only a mutt. He may look as if he's waiting to hear what he'll be called, but he sure as hell doesn't understand English.

"Can't think of a single name that's fitting," Travis said at last. "We don't want to rush this. It's got to be just the right name. You're no ordinary dog, fur face. I've got to think on it a while until I hit the right moniker."

Travis emptied the washtub, rinsed it out, and left it to dry. Together, he and the retriever went into the home they now shared.

A pampered golden gets a blow dry for its golden locks.

Simba

by Jenny Kringen

The gentle nature of the golden retriever can have a profound effect on the physical and emotional state for people in therapy or recovery from trauma. That same gentle nature even attracts a normally timid fawn.

To the untrained eye, he's just another golden retriever.

But to residents of the Minnesota Neurorehabilitation Hospital at the Brainerd Regional Human Services Center, Simba is a friend, a faithful companion and an aid in therapy and recovery.

Simba, a 2½-year-old golden retriever, is a graduate of the Canine Companions for Independence (CCI) program. CCI is a nonprofit organization formed to serve the needs of people with disabilities by providing trained dogs. Founded in 1975, CCI has four regional training centers and has trained more than 1,000 teams of students and dogs nationwide.

Mark Sell, recreation therapist at Minnesota Neurorehabilitation Hospital, first learned about CCI through a program at the Vineland facility in southern Minnesota.

"Out of all the groups I've looked at. . . CCI was rated the highest," he said.

With support from the state, Sell was selected to take a two-week class in which he learned to work with a trained dog—Simba. Simba was provided to the hospital through a grant.

Sell said he asked for the biggest golden retriever available, because "I'm really partial to golden retrievers."

After undergoing extensive interviewing, questioning and screening to ensure that he would work well with the dog, Sell returned to Brainerd in November with Simba.

Simba has adjusted well to his new surroundings and has made plenty of friends among the 35 staff members and eight to 12 patients.

Sell said Simba has given his patients a new sense of responsibility since he is everyone's dog and must be cared for by everyone. Patients take turns grooming, walking and feeding Simba.

The dog has motivated the patients to walk without assistance and has opened up the shy among them. "I think he's really doing what we wanted him to do," Sell said. "For traumatic, brain-injured people, this is something new and unusual."

Simba's effects on patients include lowered blood pressure, reduced stress and tempered emotions. Among the intricate tasks he can perform are opening and closing file cabinets, picking up credit cards off the floor with his mouth and turning a light switch on and off.

"It's hard to explain the benefits to the patients," Sell said. "But you can see [the benefits] when the dog enters a room when patients are around."

Renee, a patient at the hospital, said she enjoys having Simba around. "He's good. When we walk, he stops and looks around and waits for me," she said.

Walking in a hallway with Simba recently, Renee dropped the cane she needs. At a simple command, Simba walked over to the cane, picked it up in his mouth and gave it back to Renee.

On occasion, Simba will travel to the public library or to a restaurant with a patient. The dog is trained to wait under the table while his handlers are eating.

To ensure that Simba's life isn't all work and no play, he is taken on weekends to the homes of staff members so he can jump, run and just be a regular dog.

When CCI dogs reach 10 to 12 years of age, they are given back to the families that raised them. Simba's original family lives in Green Bay, Wis., and regularly sends him treats, toys and the occasional Green Bay Packers souvenir.

Sell noted the most important aspect of having a dog at the hospital: "They've got this innate ability to know who's in need. The thing with the dog is, he doesn't care if you walk with a limp or talk funny. Simba is nonjudgmental."

Jenny Kringen is a reporter and editor with the Brainerd (*Minn.*) Daily Dispatch *and the happy owner of a golden retriever named Chili.*

A slender golden exhibits the breed's typically featured tail on a cool autumn afternoon.

A bear of a golden dug into the snow with its face, leaving a comical frosty goatee.

Below: *What could be better than relaxing in your favorite chair with a wonderful golden retriever snuggled by your feet?*

Above: *After a roll in the snow, a golden pauses to catch its breath and throw a cockeyed look at the photographer.*
Right: *A snoozing basket of puppies laze away an autumn afternoon.*

Golden retriever puppies, with their fluffy hairdos and puppy-dog eyes, will melt the heart of the most cynical of people.

Above: *A six-year-old boy tries to get his golden to change direction while out on their daily walk.*

Above: *A golden retriever poses at twilight in front of its owner's Montana cabin.*

Left: *A golden puppy poses goofily alongside its more stoic mother.*

My Reluctant Retriever

by David Morine

 David Morine served as The Nature Conservancy's Vice President of Land Acquisition for more than eighteen years, work that resulted in the protection of 2,000 significant natural areas totaling some 3 million acres (1.2 million hectares). Now a freelance writer based in Virginia, David has written two books, *Good Dirt: Confessions of a Conservationist* and *The Class Choregus*. His writing has appeared in numerous publications, including *Field & Stream*, *American Forests*, and *Down East*. He is in the process of writing a third book, and also assists local land conservation groups with their land acquisition efforts.

Morine was also a golden retriever owner. He writes often of the antics of Percy, his curious, energetic, childlike golden, and makes it clear that the wonderful dog was very close to his heart.

"*The golden is everybody's dog—infant, kid, man, woman, grandma, everyone.*"—*Bill Tarrant,* Gun Dog Training: New Strategies from Today's Top Trainers, *1996*

Golden puppies are constantly curious and playful, but all of that activity wears young pups down, and a group nap quickly becomes the activity of the moment.

AN ELDERLY FRIEND once told me, "Everyone is entitled to one good dog." I buried mine two years ago. He was 14.

Actually, Percy wasn't mine. He much preferred my wife, and for good reason. Ruth was the one who turned my golden retriever into a pampered pet. She fed him three times a day, usually right from the table. She brushed him. She chauffeured him around. It made no difference if he was covered with mud, had rolled in manure or had just picked over a well-seasoned road kill. Percy sat right up front, with his head out the window.

We purchased Percy in the summer of 1974. He was the pick of the litter, a little ball of fluff who soon matured into a classic golden. Percy was perfect of his breed except for one—better make that two—things. First, he was sterile. When we told the breeder, she insisted on giving us half our money back. "You only got half a dog," she said with obvious disappointment. I never felt that way. Unlike most goldens, Percy had no urge to roam, which undoubtedly contributed to his longevity. No trucks come through our backyard.

Percy loved to retrieve balls: tennis balls, baseballs, softballs, anything he could get into his mouth. But he only retrieved for recreation; that was the second exception to his breed. Percy rejected retrieving as a profession right from the start. The first time I fired a gun over his head, he looked at me in terror and ran straight to Ruth. The first time I introduced Percy to water, he waded out stomach-deep, floated for a second and then paddled back to terra firma. And the first time I put him onto a live bird, he missed the point.

In truth, as a house dog Percy wasn't much better. Though I specifically banned him from the living room, almost every morning I would find him asleep on the couch. And though I specifically banned him from upstairs, almost every night I would catch him asleep on our bed.

There are many Percy stories. Most of them are about things he did wrong, the things all retrievers do wrong, such as fighting with skunks, porcupines and other dogs, or stealing pies, turkeys and hams people had left outside to cool. But the time he got into real trouble was one of the rare moments when he did what he was told.

We, like all people who feed birds, have a squirrel problem. Our problem is aggravated by the fact that I actually enjoy watching our squirrels outmaneuver the "squirrel-proof" feeders. I admire creativity, ingenuity and persistence, and there is nothing as creative, ingenious and persistent as a squirrel around a freshly filled feeder.

As a professional conservationist, however, I became concerned when our squirrels turned into a bunch of fat, lazy freeloaders. They had lost all interest in collecting nuts and were living almost exclusively on the dole. I don't like upsetting the balance of nature, so I appointed Percy the official watchdog of the feeder. Percy was touched. He took his job very seriously.

Over the years, our routine never changed. At first light, Percy would thump upstairs, where he was not allowed, and nuzzle us until we got out of bed. Then we would follow him to the sliding glass door in the kitchen. There were always at least half a dozen squirrels plundering the feeder out back.

Percy would bark and jump up and down. He was ready to go to work. At that point, we would tap the glass, open the door and watch the fun. The squirrels would be off and running at the first tap. Percy would burst through the door after them. In his younger days, he would actually shinny two or three feet up the big beech tree to which the squirrels always retreated. Thanks to our warning there was no way that Percy could make a kill. But he never lost heart; the next morning, he would be upstairs nuzzling us and ready to go.

All was well until Ruth's 85-year-old grandmother came for a visit. Tillie was deaf, but refused to wear her hearing aid. Otherwise, she was in wonderful shape. On the first night of Tillie's visit, Ruth finally decided to enforce the "no Percy upstairs" rule. The last thing anybody wanted was Percy nuzzling Tillie. That meant Percy was not nuzzling us; we overslept.

When we finally got up I realized I was going to be late for an important meeting. I quickly showered, shaved and got dressed while Ruth made the bed and cleaned up after me. It wouldn't do for Tillie to think she was a lousy housekeeper. Percy was forgotten. I had to get going, and Ruth was trying to coordinate her plans for the day.

Percy, confused, followed us to the front door. When it opened, he was out like a flash.

The squirrels out front never knew what hit them. They were industrious, but definitely much dumber than the backyard band. These squirrels eked out an honest living by collecting acorns that dropped from the big oak. They had never raided the bird feeder and never participated in the morning routine. They had also never seen Percy all fired up. To them, he was the gentle slob who spent his day lying on the front stoop licking tennis balls—about as threatening as a stone.

Their first reaction was to freeze, which gave Percy a tremendous advantage. When they finally figured out that this charging mass of teeth and golden fur was after them, they broke for the oak. All of them made it, except for one. This little fellow decided to hightail it down the driveway.

Percy never looked more noble than when he pranced back to the house proudly displaying his prize. He had done his job.

He was totally confused when Ruth whacked him on the side of the head. It was the first and only time that Ruth ever struck Percy. "Percy, you bad dog!" she yelled. "Drop that squirrel!" The poor little thing desperately tried to crawl to the big oak, but its hind legs refused to work. Its spine had been snapped.

"I'd better get my gun and put it out of its misery," I said. Tillie came downstairs just as I was loading up. "Going hunting?" she inquired brightly.

Apparently the sight of me, dressed in a suit, loading my shotgun, did not seem strange to Tillie. She was from New Jersey and must have figured that this was what all Virginia gentlemen did each day before they went off to work. What could I say? I didn't have time to explain, plus Tillie wouldn't be able to hear me anyway. "Yes," I said, and ran back out.

I dispatched the squirrel and buried him deep in the woods where I was sure Percy wouldn't find him. Ruth was still lecturing Percy when I came back to the kitchen.

Tillie had settled down with a cup of tea. "Get anything?" she asked cheerily.

"One squirrel," I replied, holding up a finger.

"Good," said Tillie, sipping her tea.

I'm positive Tillie went to her grave thinking that I routinely shot a squirrel before going to the office. She told Ruth that Art, Ruth's grandfather, used to shoot squirrels that robbed their feeder, too. "That was in the old days, before New Jersey got all built-up," she noted.

Ruth is putting pressure on me to get another dog. I'm resisting. Then again, I see a new generation of fat, lazy squirrels freeloading from my latest squirrel-proof feeder. They don't budge when I tap on the sliding glass door. Maybe it's time to reestablish the balance of nature.

Facing page: *As if posing for a senior picture, this golden adolescent is about as cute as they come.*

Guardian

by Michael J. Rosen

Though travel keeps Penn from ownership, he dog-sits
a golden retriever named—or misnamed—"Angel"
the weekends her owners sail at their summer home.
They furnish Penn with toys, her rations, a leash,
the six commands that govern Angel's world,
and a lengthy list of, well, recommendations.

His neighbors' gratitude matches his own.
Penn's missed the dogs—not one, but the continuing
presence of Dog that ran through their lives,
out an unlocked gate, and on to somewhere
misnamed "a good home." The dogs were guests;
they stole the family's hearts like a set of towels.

These days, Penn is the visitor at his home,
a man whose comings and goings he greets himself.
People who think they know, prescribe a pet
for Penn, threaten to surprise him with a dog.
Once, on his own, Penn parked outside the pound,
between trash cans a third-grade class had painted
with the bright, mournful faces of kittens and pups,
and two crowds of letters that Penn mistook
at first, PREVENT LITTERS, then understood.
(He mistook the tears, too, as he backed out,
and how they came surprised from him, from kennels
of grief abandoned by the breeze of getting on.)

Angel adopts her temporary master
so heartily it still embarrasses Penn
to take it personally. Nudging his hand,
delivering toys, the dog has taught this man
which ones to throw and which to pull, where
to scratch and to walk, and how a bed is shared.

"On Sunday, Angel turns nine," the neighbors tell Penn
as they leave. "That's sixty-three in human years,"
the woman explains, bestowing on the dog a kiss
that's clearly human enough. "We've never missed
a birthday before. So Angel's counting on you
to celebrate a little. Just you two."

Penn's been suspicious of equivalents:
One's weight on the moon. Miles of matchsticks
laid end to end. Centigrade. Metrics.
Or multiplying a canine's age by seven,
demonstrating some human factor to redress
the pet's prodigal slice of the heart's pie.

Arithmetic can't make something what it's not,
but then, it did make Penn a businessman.
It won't make Angel a man—no, a woman—
nor an angel, however sweetly guardian-
like she is hovering over, watching Penn
with needle, iron, paring knife, and pills.

Penn himself turns sixty-three on Friday.
Coincidence, on the other hand, he trusts:
it's the unfair happening alongside the fair.
Though man and dog begin this weekend like others,
within a leash's length, exploring a street
that Penn had only known from stories above

and his assigned parking space beneath,
Penn does attempt to find something special
for the dog's day, a treat befitting her years.
In the driver's seat, Angel waits while Penn
surveys the costly ham- or chocolate-flavoured,
indestructible English rubber chews.

She promptly halved the ring on the ride home,
intently consumed it all before bed,
and woke Penn heaving it up on the quilt at dawn.
The rest of their time, Penn dreams of his own presents—
birthday, retirement, the chance for a dog of his own.
His first, really. Not the children's or the neighbor's . . .

a companion to grow old—at least, older—
beside. 63 + 12 years
with a devoted . . . 84-year-old dog,
(Isn't a mutt's lifespan even longer?)
would make Penn 75. Another dog?
A dozen years? Penn at 87?

Such health, such luck, such foolish accounting aside,
could Penn survive the whole housebreaking,
heartbreaking shebang again? "Ask me
in a year," Penn says to Angel, stroking her thick,
thickening coat, celebrating this weekend
that love so happened to litter his way.

Michael J. Rosen is the editor of In the Company of
Dogs, *from which this excerpt was taken.*

*A golden in the house fills your home
with love.*

Above: *In need of an ottoman for its tail, a golden retriever thoroughly takes over an unoccupied chair.*

Left: *Many will argue that golden retrievers are the most beautiful dogs in the world. These two handsome goldens only further that argument.*

PART II

Golden Days

"Handsome, good tempered, intelligent and aware of your every need, [golden retrievers] give more pleasure than you can possibly return."
Marigold Timson, A Dog Owner's Guide
to Golden Retrievers, *1989*

Above: *Goldens have powerful, athletic bodies built for a rapid retrieve, though you may not be in any particular hurry to get your knawed-up stick back.*
Left: *To share part of your life with a golden retriever is to live a little better.*

Sports Afield with a Golden Receiver

by Timothy Foote

 To share part of your life with a golden retriever is to live a little better; the details of life seem more vivid with a beautiful golden by your side. Days with the dog, days which seem mundane at the surface, resonate with love, happiness—with meaning.

Timothy Foote is a journalist by trade and a golden retriever fan by inclination. A former Paris-based foreign correspondent and a senior editor for *Time* magazine, Foote has served as a senior editor and writer at *Smithsonian* magazine for the last decade. He previously taught writing courses at Yale and Stanford, and has published two books, one for children entitled *The Great Ringtail Garbage Caper* about raccoons that hijack a garbage truck. He also edited a collection of dog stories by his father, John Taintor Foote, entitled *Dumb-bell of Brookfield, Pocono Shot and Other Great Dog Stories.*

When Foote describes Pamela, the golden in this story, he speaks with great affection. "She had amazing energy, courage, almost inexhaustible affection plus a sense of play and what seemed to be a sense of humor," he wrote. "I went miles and miles in the woods with her and have never known a like comradeship." Pamela also had a fondness for chasing tennis balls, and Foote's seemingly mundane subject matter, an afternoon in the park playing "tennis-ball football" with Pamela, is filled with the love and enthusiasm inherent in any owner–golden retriever relationship.

A beautiful golden retriever stands in a snowy field.

IF ANYBODY SHOULD wander onto the back trails of Washington's Rock Creek Park and glimpse an apparently demented man clapping his hands together and shouting "Bravo! Bravo!" there's no need to reach for a stick or run. It'll be me. And if you look out ahead you will see a big golden retriever barreling along, with a kind of proud, shoulder-rolling trot, benignly seeming to conduct the world with her tail.

That'll be Pamela just after making an over-the-shoulder circus catch of a tennis ball. When she fetches it back she sometimes gets a bit of dog biscuit. Meanwhile, extravagant applause is in order, and "Bravo!"—which it took me a lot of time in Paris to learn to shout without feeling like a sap—does as well for dogs as divas.

⁂ ⁂ ⁂

The game we're playing is simple: at a hand gesture, the dog tears away into the middle distance; the man throws a tennis-ball pass; the dog snaffles it up on the first bounce at a dead run and proudly paces toward an imaginary end zone. It can be played on lawns, vacant lots, even (with caution) on the tops of aircraft carriers. But for pigskin fans and aging high school passers it is best and briskest if practiced during pro football season in the woods where—I'll be the first to admit it—successful completions require breathtaking accuracy and amazing eye-mouth coordination.

Indeed, it is sometimes hard not to think of Pamela as a kind of four-footed Drew Pearson (the wide receiver, that is). She's a lot quicker than Pearson, of course. Especially when it comes to that final lunge for the ball, a lightning forward strike of the head and neck, the kind of last-second, snaky stroke that in the water lets retrievers suddenly clamp down on an elusive duck.

What I throw these days is mostly long, high floaters that might put Walter Mitty in mind not of Pearson's teammate Roger Staubach but of Earl Morrall and the late Baltimore Colts.

By wonderful coincidence, that is just what the game calls for. If you want a long completion on a wooded path, you have to loft the ball up through tree branches, calculating to a nicety, so it will sail down to Earth without being deflected by leaves. Doing this is most challenging when the path ahead is twisty and the dog is running at full speed.

Winter is easier. Those arching throws float through the bare, black branches, to fall just ahead of the galloping receiver, sometimes bouncing so perfectly that she seems to inhale the ball going flat out. But sometimes she has to lunge to left or right, or leap to get the ball with all four feet off the ground like a sort of fur-trimmed flying carpet.

Of course I don't have to throw with hundreds of pounds of bone and muscle bearing down on me. But Pamela runs a gauntlet that is the moral equivalent of Redskin linebackers—hairpin turns in the path, bushes, stumps, brush piles, fallen trees. Imagine running

Like siblings standing (or sitting) at attention in front of authority to hide mischief going on just under the surface, these beautiful goldens sit for their master.

Timothy Foote's Pamela, like this golden, had a particular fondness for tennis balls. Foote and Pamela often played "tennis-ball football" during the fall, a sport requiring "amazing eye-mouth coordination," something the talented Pamela had in spades.

flat out down a twisting path, as bumpy as the Mikado's billiard table, and then catching a ball in your mouth. In her situation, I figure, even a Pearson might poke out an eye on the end of some protruding stick or splatter himself against a tree (trees never get called for interference in our game).

What thrower does not remember passes thrown long or dropped by some other kid? But anything Pamela can lay a tooth on she can catch, even if she has to produce the kind of diving, rolling reception that you sometimes see made in the end zone, about ten inches off the ground, on a short, flat pass thrown after the receiver is already diving through the air.

If there is a sift of snow when she does that, she kicks up an explosion of powder and leaves, rolls over and grins. And the dog-loving passer is reminded of a famous trainer's line about great racehorses: "They run from the heart, like children at play."

I fantasize at times about inventing Retriever Football-Tennis. Or even creating a Golden Baseball League with a designated hitter (human) and dogs fielding and running bases. (The late Bill Veeck would be the commissioner of choice.) Certainly Pamela would never hold out for more pay or threaten to play in Calgary next year.

She might chase squirrels, though. Her approach is as full of folly as Pickett's Charge. Any squirrel, no matter how far off, no matter how much cover she could use to stalk it, tends to bring a straight frontal assault. She would make a lousy tackler. Once a squirrel let her get between him and the only tree for 20 yards around. The squirrel just swung a hip to the right, drawing the gullible dog that way, then zipped past Pam and up the tree. Alas, she has never heard my old coach (and math teacher) Tiny Nordstrom yelling "Follow the man, not the ball!"

❧ ❧ ❧

The command "Drop it" she sometimes takes under advisement—hoping I will produce a scrap of dog biscuit. Sometimes, after a spectacular effort, as when, with a high bouncing ball, she bongs it up in the air with the tip of her nose first, like a seal, before making a showboat catch, I whistle her back to a huddle, I kneel. She sits. We talk in low tones about the next play. Sometimes I rub her ears and tell her she's the most beautiful and skillful dog in the world. This is no more than the truth, but she is always pleased to hear it. At such times she looks at me with total attention and loving brown eyes. Her glance, however, has a way of shifting toward the pocket where the biscuits are.

An owner gives a much-appreciated tummy rub to her deliciously happy golden.

Above: *This sleepy golden certainly doesn't mind duty as an ottoman, nor does its owner mind a warm place to rest his tired feet.*

Right: *Spring flowers bloom in brilliant yellow, but this golden—in the tradition of generations of dogs before it—sees the flower field as something to romp through while returning from a fetch.*

Above: *A golden puppy positions itself perfectly for effortless refreshment on a hot summer day.*
Left: *A puppy defensively reels from the onslaught of a sibling that has an insatiable desire to make the rope toy its own.*

Above: *Three golden puppies redefine adorable as they pose on a saddle in the American West.*
Left: *A pudgy nine-week-old puppy enjoys a hearty hug from its owner.*

Lily's Gift

by Karyn Kay Zweifel

 Karyn Kay Zweifel weaves the supernatural into her many short stories. By adding some golden retriever puppies, she has quite a story indeed. The author of three books of ghost stories, *Southern Vampires, Covered Bridge Ghost Stories,* and *Dog-Gone Ghost Stories,* Zweifel makes her home in Birmingham, Alabama.

This story, from *Dog-Gone Ghost Stories,* floats between two worlds—perhaps past and present, perhaps something else—telling the tale of Lily and her boy Willy in one world and the story of Janie and her family in another. Through the whimperings of newborn goldens, these two worlds unite.

With such patience and loyalty—not to mention gorgeous looks—a golden and its owner bond very closely.

THE BOY'S LIP quivered—it was clear he was about to break out in disgraceful, heaving sobs. "Give it back," he demanded, barely choking out the words. He was no more than nine, but his defiant posture, legs spread wide and hands on hips, was the mirror image of the older boys tormenting him.

"You can't make me," singsonged the ringleader, holding the precious leather glove high above his head.

Willy stood still, feeling as if his feet were weighted by concrete. He was unwilling to jump up and try to snatch the glove away, certain the bully would only raise it higher.

"Give it to me," he repeated stubbornly. "Or else . . ."

"Or else what, baby?" Another boy taunted him. "You gonna cry to Mommy?"

Just then a golden fury came cannonballing down the street. In an instant she was leaping, growling, and generally terrorizing the three older boys, while Willy looked on in astonishment. An instant later the tormentors were gone, and Lily sat in front of her master with his baseball glove laying neatly between her front paws. Her tongue was fully extended in a most unladylike manner, and she grinned up at the boy as if to say, "Did I do good, Master?"

He threw himself down and wrapped his arms around her neck. There wasn't far to go because he was not especially tall—but the dog was. "Lily, you saved me! Oh, Lily, you're the very best dog there ever was!"

She diligently swiped his face all over with her tongue, effectively cleaning the soot and grime that had collected there during his long and circuitous route home from school. Then she stood and frisked around him, her tail held high, dashing this way and that, sometimes leaning low on her front paws and swishing her tail in an invitation to mischief. Short, high barks communicated her message: "I've been home all alone, all day, and there are so many garbage cans to investigate and places to see and people to sniff! Get a move on, will you?"

"Willy! That you?" the boy's mother called as she leaned out the window and looked down the street. She recognized the substance of the dog's yelping if not the actual content. Willy scooped up his glove and trotted down the street, Lily close behind.

"Go 'round to the butcher's, will you, and get a pound of burger for dinner tonight. Tell him to charge it."

"Can I get Lily a bone, Mama?"

The woman shrugged and smiled. "Why not? Come directly home with it now, so I can start dinner!"

Willy opened the door to the stairs that led up to their first-floor apartment and tossed the baseball glove up the stairs, where it landed safely in the shadows on the first landing. Whistling—unnecessarily—for Lily to follow, he skipped down the street and around the corner, his encounter with the older boys totally forgotten.

⚘ ⚘ ⚘

Janie tucked the blanket tightly up against the girls' chins and planted a kiss on each forehead. "Sleep, now," she said firmly. "To-morrow we'll get you started at your new school." Two pairs of round, slightly frightened eyes stared back at her.

"Everything will be fine," she assured them before ducking under the sheet that was tacked up across the little alcove, which opened out directly into the spacious living room. The windows in the apartment were still uncurtained, and the Chicago night was anything but dark—a row of streetlights illuminated the windows as brightly as daylight. Silently demanding attention, stacks of boxes confronted Janie, but she successfully ignored them. Instead, she collapsed on the sofa in front of the television, keeping the volume low so it wouldn't wake any of the sleeping children.

With that uncanny sense of hearing mothers seem to develop, she sensed the girls whispering beyond the sheet. "Go to sleep, now, girls," she said sternly. "I mean it!"

The noise subsided, and Janie lost herself in another episode of *Marcus Welby, MD.* It was twenty minutes before another sound registered on her acute second sense. It was a whining, snuffling sound, so faint she almost missed it. One of her girls was crying, Janie thought as she jumped up and twisted the television knob, cutting off the singers extolling the virtues of Gulf Oil in mid-verse. Tiptoeing quietly to the alcove, she gently lifted a corner of the temporary curtain.

Just enough light spilled in to reveal the softly rounded faces of her two daughters, nine and ten years old, relaxed in sleep. A little spit bubble had formed at the corner of Angie's mouth, and Carol was snoring softly—but there was no sign of distress on either face.

The bond between a child and the family golden retriever is very strong, and the trust is readily apparent in the sleeping forms of a seven-year-old and his golden.

Janie shrugged. It had been a long, hard day—well, really, a long, hard week getting herself and her five children moved to Chicago, finding this apartment, getting furniture set up, and utilities turned on. So maybe she was imagining things, but there was nothing wrong with her that a little sleep wouldn't cure. She turned off the living room lamps, reducing the unpacked boxes to mere shadows. Then she stood for a moment and admired the graceful symmetry of windows in the main room of this fine old apartment

Teething golden retriever puppies like to get their mouths around anything chewable. A leather bone suits this youngster quite nicely.

before heading back through the kitchen to her own room.

❧ ❧ ❧

The room was dim. All four windows across the face of the long formal living room were draped in swathes of lace and thick fabric that collected dust. When Willy hid in the curtains or pushed them aside to look out at the street, a fine, nearly invisible cloud arose and made him sneeze violently.

Right now he wasn't looking out the window—he was trapped, sitting on a little chair while his mother and her friends chattered on and on. The light clattering of teacups on saucers provided a perfect counterpoint to the women's casual tones. But listening closer, Willy was appalled at the horrific subject matter.

"Had to have it all taken out, dear, scraped her out like a melon."

"After the baby was born, she never walked upright again. Stooped over and scurried, like a crab, she was. . ."

Willy's face must have revealed his distaste. His mother, glancing over at him, snickered and then quickly covered her mouth with her hand. "Willy, dear, would you like to go outside and play?"

With great relief he nodded and sidled out of the room in no time flat. He poked his head into the curtained alcove that served as his room to pick up his glove and call softly for Lily, who was lying patiently on the little rag rug by the side of his bed. They scampered out the front door, Willy waving to acknowledge his mother's automatic "Be careful!"

Outside it was a perfect spring Saturday. The sky was as blue as blue can be, with just a few high, thin clouds hurrying by. The breeze was light and playful, and Willy could smell the heavy scent of fish and water from the lake a half mile to the east. In just two short hours, the sharp crack of the bat and the roar of the fans would resound from the confines of Wrigley Field, and Willy was determined to be there.

"C'mon, Lily," he urged as he broke out into a half trot. Wrigley Field was two blocks away, and if they got there soon enough, they could squeeze through a hole in the fence and hide out under the stands until the game began. The bigger boys had bragged about it. Willy had found the hole last week, and he and Lily had spent a glorious twenty minutes exploring the darkened, empty stands before a prowling watchman had sent them hurrying back to squeeze under the fence. Today Willy was going to try sneaking in to catch the Cubs playing.

He stopped running when he got to the field, put his hands behind his back and strolled nonchalantly, lips puckered up to whistle. The sight of a big, tall policeman made a shiver run deliciously down his spine. Lily, always game for an adventure, trotted obediently by his side. Once around the corner, he began to scan the fence, looking anxiously for the remembered opening.

There it was—half hidden by a tall weed growing out of crack in the pavement. Willy dropped to his knees and wiggled through in a flash. Still on his belly, he called softly to Lily.

"Come on, girl, you can do it!" he held out his hand to encourage her. She whimpered just a bit and scratched at the concrete with one front paw. When he called again, she cried a little louder and dropped to her stomach, trying to pull herself through the opening with a frantic scrabbling motion of her front and back paws.

She couldn't fit. She squeezed and wiggled, crying softly all the while, but her rear half would not make it under the fence without getting caught on the jagged edges of the loose fence wire.

"Don't think she's going to make it, boy," a booming voice said in a conversational, relaxed tone. Willy tensed, raising himself into a half-crouch and staring up. It was the burly policeman from around the corner.

"May I?" With a gesture that was almost courtly, the policeman offered his arm to Willy. Stunned, the boy reached up and was hauled to his feet.

"Pretty dog," the officer commented as the man and the boy walked briskly to the gate. Barking shrilly every few feet, Lily was tracking their progress on the outside of the fence. "She a golden retriever?"

Willy could only nod dumbly in reply. At the gate, the officer bent over to look Willy straight in the face. "Don't do this again, young man," he cautioned. "You're getting off light this time. But if you try it again, I'm warning you, it won't go so easy!"

Willy hung his head. "Yes, sir," he replied, in a voice scarcely loud enough to be heard. On the sidewalk outside, Lily hung her head too.

The day was too delightful to spend long in regrets. Out of sight of the baseball field, Lily's tail rose high like a flag again, and Willy's spirits rose to match. Finding discarded treasures at every turn, they picked their way through the alleyways. Lily even scared up a few cats scavenging for their dinners and thoroughly enjoyed the subsequent chase.

On the last chase Willy laughed so hard that his stomach ached. Lily managed to comer a scrawny, ferocious-looking cat, who stood with its back arched, spitting fiercely at the big, barking dog. Lily turned to look at Willy, as if to say, "What on earth do I do now?" He howled with laughter, and Lily, her pride hurt, stalked off in the opposite direction and lay with her head on her paws. The cat abruptly sat down and began to wash its face as if nothing at all unusual had happened.

After a couple hours of roaming, Willy noticed the wind

picking up. Ugly gray clouds were scudding in fast from the lake. The shirt sleeves that were perfectly adequate at noon now felt skimpy, so he called to Lily and headed home.

His mother's friends were fortunately all gone so he could sit in the warm kitchen and recount his adventures to his mother—an edited version, of course. He spoke between bites of the delicate finger sandwiches left over from the afternoon tea party. Lily lay at his feet and watched hopefully for any crumbs that might fall.

"She's getting fat, Mama," Willy complained. "I think we're feeding her too much."

Without a word, his mother dropped to her knees and gently patted Lily's abdomen. A shake of her head was the only reply. Then, puzzling Willy even further, she fetched the jug of milk from the icebox, filled a bowl, and set it down in front of Lily. As the dog drank, both the boy and his mother watched her with love in their eyes.

❧ ❧ ❧

Janie had a bag of groceries on her hip and two in her hands while she pawed through her purse for the key. The door on the street

It's amazing there is any water left in the stream this golden retriever just emerged from.

level slammed, and she heard footsteps ascending the dark stairs. It was Mrs. May, the upstairs neighbor.

"Let me help you, dear," she cooed. "Got your hands full?" She relieved Janie of two bags of groceries, freeing Janie's hands to fit the key into the battered old lock.

"Would you like a cup of coffee, Mrs. May?" Janie asked politely but hoped the woman would refuse. She had a lot to do, and she needed to leave in an hour to pick up the children.

"Oh, no, I couldn't." The woman was peering around, looking in every corner and cocking her head as if to hear some faint sound.

"Is something wrong?"

"No, no." Now the woman was peeking into the grocery bags.

"What is it, Mrs. May?" Janie spoke more sharply than she had intended.

"I just don't want you to get in trouble," the woman blurted. "I know how the landlord feels about dogs!"

Now Janie was thoroughly confused. "What dogs?"

The look her neighbor gave her was full of pity. "You can't hide it, dear. You'll have to give them up, or else the landlord will have you evicted. It's happened before!"

"Give what up?"

Now the older lady leaned close, a fellow conspirator. "You can trust me, honey," she whispered. "I just love puppies. I'd have one myself if I could!"

"Look, Mrs. May. I don't have a dog, I don't have any puppies, and I don't want any trouble, okay?" Janie picked up the groceries and stalked back to the kitchen. She stopped dead in her tracks, Mrs. May nearly treading on her heels, as an explanation occurred to her.

"You've heard them too!" she cried.

Mrs. May gleefully clapped her hands. "Now will you let me see them? How many are there? Where's their mother, poor darlings?"

Janie shook her head. "There are no puppies." Mrs. May's face fell. "But if you want to come down here at about ten o'clock tonight, I'd like you to hear something." Now it was Mrs. May's turn to look puzzled.

"Will you do that for me?" Janie asked, gently propelling the woman toward the door.

"Certainly, dear, I'd be glad to. But the puppies. . ."

Janie put on a big grin. "Ten o'clock," she repeated as she softly shut the door.

Mrs. May's reply was faint beyond the door. "Ten o'clock."

Janie hastily ran all five children through the bathtub, feeling like the foreman on an assembly line as she checked behind their ears and issued clean underwear. By ten o'clock the older ones were at least quiet in their rooms, and her two youngest girls were snuggled up together fast asleep in the little alcove.

A tentative knock on the door came at five after the hour. "Oh, my dear, I don't mean to make a pest out of myself," Mrs. May began, but Janie shushed her.

"Let's just have a nice cup of tea and watch the evening news, shall we?"

They hadn't been sitting for more than five minutes before the whimpering began. It was soft, not at all panic-stricken, and it immediately brought a smile to both women's faces.

"Oh, can I go see them?" Mrs. May was halfway to her feet.

Janie, still smiling, just nodded. They crossed the living room and pulled the curtain to the alcove aside, letting light from the room spill into every corner. The smile of anticipation on Mrs. May's face faded away as her head swiveled this way and that.

"Where are they?" She forgot to whisper, and one of the girls stirred uneasily in her sleep.

Janie shrugged, holding up her empty hands. Mrs. May got down on her knees, every joint cracking, and lifted a corner of the bedspread to look under the bed. Slowly, awkwardly, she stood up. Janie had backed up into the living room, watching her neighbor carefully.

"That is the creepiest thing, I declare." The garrulous woman was almost speechless.

"I'm glad you heard them, too. Sometimes the girls hear the puppies before they go to sleep, but it doesn't scare them."

"Well," Mrs. May admitted, "it's not really a scary or creepy thing. They don't sound sad at all."

"Do you believe me now when I say we don't have any puppies?"

Mrs. May could only nod, a little shamefaced at her earlier insistence on the puppies' existence.

"I wonder where they came from?" Janie mused aloud as she escorted Mrs. May out the door. "And why would we hear them cry now?"

Mama and her doubly-warm six-day-old puppies relax by an evening fire.

❧ ❧ ❧

Lily was going crazy. She would run a few feet in one direction, her toenails skidding on the highly polished floor, and then turn around and run the other direction, whining and yipping with every step. Sometimes she would cower close to the floor, looking up with wild

Breeders, show judges, and everyday owners of goldens all agree that the kind temperament of the golden retriever is the hallmark of the breed.

eyes at Willy, begging him to do something.

"What is it, girl?" He pleaded with her to tell him what was wrong, but she could not obey this time. Willy's mother was upstairs visiting the neighbor, and he was frantic.

When he found a drop of bloody water on the floor, his panic reached new heights. Now Lily was panting so hard she barely had time to whine, and she lay next to his bed on the little rug she'd claimed as her own three years ago as a puppy. Her abdomen heaved and rolled alarmingly, seeming to have a life of its own. Willy watched with terrified eyes.

Finally Lily raised her head and let loose a howl that set his teeth on edge. Willy began to howl and cry too, his tears flowing even faster when she growled at his outstretched hand.

A key in the lock sounded like salvation. It was his mother, and she bustled in the door calling out his name. She had heard Lily's howl upstairs in the neighbor's kitchen.

"Willy," she said, "go get me a couple of old sheets from the rag bag. Then fetch my sewing scissors from the basket in the kitchen." She was rolling up her sleeves as she talked. "And an apron from the drawer."

"What's wrong with Lily, Mama?" He was gasping between sobs.

"She'll be fine," she replied briskly. "Do what I tell you—now!"

A warm spot snuggled in a flannel blanket is a wonderful place for a little snooze.

Willy collected everything, his ears tuned to the turmoil in the alcove. His mother was in there now speaking softly to Lily, who whimpered in reply but did not growl. He thrust the sheets, scissors, and apron through a gap in the curtain and slipped outside, too scared to watch whatever mysterious ritual was happening on the floor by his bed.

In an hour, it was all over. Lily's yelps of pain had reached a crescendo and then slowed, finally stopping altogether. Willy's mother came from behind the curtain, her hands held high and smeared with a thick, curious layer of reddish-black gore.

"Go on in, Willy," she said softly. "Lily's got a surprise for you."

❧ ❧ ❧

The reflected light of the candles danced on the windowpanes, and Janie felt her heart swell with the warmth of family and friends surrounding her. "Happy birthday, to you. . ." The sweet strains were a little off-key, and the birthday cake was undeniably lopsided, but the candles burned with a bright optimism. Her children sang with enthusiasm and unbidden tears rose to her eyes.

"Now for the biggest surprise of all, Mama," Angie said, and, leading Janie into the living room, she flung aside the curtain to the alcove with a flourish.

"Oh, Eddie!" It was her baby brother, all the way from South Carolina to celebrate her birthday. Now the tears began in earnest, and her brother laughed as he held her.

"Such a bad surprise that I made you cry, eh?"

Janie wiped her face with her sleeve (a gesture her oldest son stored away in his mind for future use as a defense), and the seven of them sat down to birthday cake.

The children went to bed, protesting mildly, at eleven o'clock, and Janie had her brother all to herself for a precious few hours. They talked till two, when Janie brought out sheets and a pillow to make up a bed on the sofa.

"We'll try not to wake you up in the morning," she promised. "The kids all leave for school at 7:30, so it'll be quiet after that."

Eddie unwound himself from the sheet and blanket at ten the next morning, moaning loudly and mock-staggering into the kitchen to find his sister.

"Coffee, Janie, coffee!" he moaned. "This is the noisiest house I ever slept in!"

Janie grinned as she poured him a cup, black and strong from several hours of stewing. She spoke over her shoulder as she rinsed out the pot and refilled it to make a fresh pot.

"What do you mean? The kids bother you?"

"No, I'm talking about those confounded puppies. They sounded like they were under my pillow."

"They weren't far—they're in the alcove."

He looked startled and then grimaced as he tasted the coffee. "Oohh, boy, this is bad!" He pushed the cup away. "When did you all get a dog?"

Janie's grin grew wider. "We didn't."

"You'll have to explain yourself. I'm just a country bumpkin."

With a tongue seemingly designed for slathering over a boy's ice cream cone, a golden licks its chops within range of its strawberry target.

She shrugged. "I can't explain it. Just sometimes, at night, we hear puppies cry. They're right there, in that little alcove, but we can't see them."

Eddie shivered. "Doesn't it scare you?"

"Not really. You weren't scared, were you?"

He considered for a moment. "Nah. Are you sure it's not your

Puppy siblings with gravity-defying tails trot across a yard in search of new mischief.

neighbors though?"

She shook her head, definite. "No, the upstairs neighbor was ready to get me evicted over the noise because she heard it too. And the closest building is way too far away to hear it that clearly. You said yourself, it's right there, right in the living room."

"Weird—very weird. But it suits you." Janie swiped at him with a dish towel, and he ducked, his grin matching hers. "Is that coffee ready yet?"

⁓ ⁓ ⁓

Willy tiptoed into the alcove, full of fear but also filled with faith in his mother's goodwill. Lily was curled up in a rough nest of torn strips of sheet, and her tail thumped lightly when she saw his face. She looked up at him, her eyes filled with unquestioning trust.

In the half circle formed by her furry, golden torso, five misshapen lumps were staggering about on uncertain little legs. They butted up against each other and against Lily's neck and legs, searching blindly for her belly and her swollen nipples.

Willy's mouth dropped open in awe. Lily, watching his reaction, seemed to smile fondly at him. At last each of the five pups found a place, and their thin, mewing cries were stilled. Crouching next to his dog, Willy breathed a promise: "Oh, Lily, what a wonderful dog you are. I will remember this forever."

⁓ ⁓ ⁓

Janie was curled up on the sofa with a book. The house was quiet, peaceful. It was the kind of moment filled with an ordered sense of contentment that sustained her through all the other hours of chaos and disorder. Beyond her in the alcove she heard small whimpering noises of puppies looking for—and finding—sustenance, and the sound made her smile. It sounded like hope fulfilled.

Above: *"Golden" retrievers come in a variety of shades. A reddish coat is quite common, while others sport more of a honey-colored look.*
Facing page: *An adorable golden pup mugs for the camera on a Technicolor autumn day.*

Jeremy

by Roger Caras

Like Jeremy, this golden is an excellent stick retriever.

Retrievers have a remarkable built-in computing system that is tied to what may be close to being the best eyesight in the dog world. You can take [my golden retriever] Jeremy out on the beach behind our house and throw a stick. It doesn't matter how high or how far you throw it, and if there is any daylight left at all. Jeremy is under this stick when it comes down. He handles parabolas, altitudes, speed, and EPI (expected point of impact) like a multi-eyed computerized machine. If he could hit, the ball clubs would be after him. Retrievers are incredible outfielders.

Jeremy's fielding ability led to a strange confrontation a few years back. Six-month-old Yankee, a perfectly splendid bloodhound puppy, joined us in 1975. Jeremy was already mature, and Yankee accepted, as his genes insisted he must, the dominant male already in place. But since Jeremy was a retriever, Yankee assumed he must be, too. They were exercised together along with several of the other dogs, and Yankee pounded on down the beach with the best of them after the airborne stick. Problem, though: A bloodhound can't see beans in a pan. They don't have to, since they can smell a single bean a mile away. Yankee was never under the stick when it came down except by accident, and then it was usually to have it land on his head. Jeremy's elegant midair pirouettes to snatch the stick a few feet before impact were simply not in the bloodhound repertoire. A lost stick in heavy growth was a cinch for Yankee to find by smell, but not when it was sailing overhead.

But time plays tricks on all of us, and the trick it played on Jeremy was in the form of a submissive puppy that wouldn't stop growing. At eight months Yankee, the flop-eared klutz, was bigger then Jeremy, and at ten months he was pushy. The time finally came when Jeremy would catch the stick and Yankee would tug it away from him and run to home base for the reward, leaving the poor air dancer Jeremy standing looking dejected and cheated, which, indeed, he had been.

Ah, but all that breeding for guaranteed performance in the field was not for naught. Jeremy finally outwitted Yankee. He would pound on down the flat and catch the stick with his usually superb elevation, twist and snatch, and then immediately head for the nearest beach plum. Up went the leg and the letter was mailed. Yankee, a male, too, of course, would come bounding along intent on stealing the stick and the thunder when he would encounter Jeremy in the act of marking that bush. Some things in a dog rise above even the desire to gain praise. Yankee had absolutely no choice. A male had sent a message, and he, as a male, had to answer it. Waiting his turn, he would mark on top of Jeremy's mark while Jeremy shot back to headquarters with the prize. Poor Yankee was locked into place. He stood there helpless, peeing with the silliest look on his face as he lost out time and again. Jeremy was triumphant. Wondrously they are still very good friends today, long after the stick throwing has stopped. Yankee has a heart condition and Jeremy's hips hurt him, so they spend most of their time, I guess, remembering. (I am not absolutely certain of this, but it seems to me that once Jeremy had worked out his keep-the-stick technique he would take a long drink of water just before an exercise session.)

Roger Caras is the President of the American Society for the Prevention of Cruelty to Animals and the author of seventy books on animals and the environment, including A Celebration of Dogs, *from which this excerpt was taken.*

Below: *A golden retriever brings yet another "present" to its owner, who is likely standing next to a pile of sticks reminiscent of a beaver lodge.*
Overleaf: *A pup playfully sniffs its mother in a field of dandelions.*

Above: *Looking quite beautiful while posing for this shot, this golden probably has come across this fire hydrant before, looking not so perfect and exhibiting a little less respect for the fire plug.*

"Few breeds can match the golden's friendly, loving, and gentle nature; fewer still display its innate love for children."
—*Jamie J. Sucher,* Golden Retrievers, *1987*

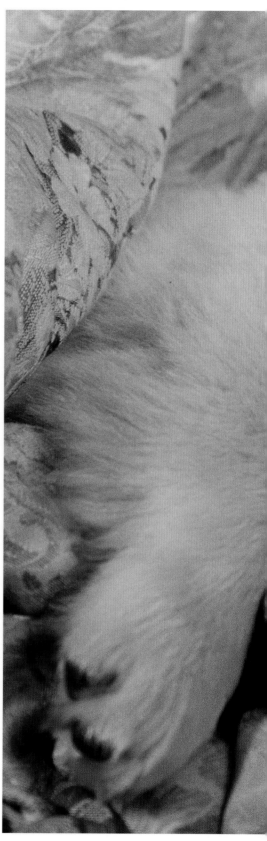

Above: *"In disposition the Golden is kindly, gentle, and utterly faithful; he has great sagacity, endurance and pluck, is tractable, capable of great self-control, assimilates quickly and remembers well. He can learn anything his owner cares to teach him. . . . He is exceptionally free from the ordinary 'doggy' vulgarities, in fact the epithet applied to Champion Noranby Camp-fire applies to the breed as a whole 'A great gentleman.'"—W. M. Charlesworth,* Golden Retrievers, *1952*

A golden puppy has found a comfy bed to catch a few Zs.

Above: *As with any dog—particularly very active ones like golden retrievers—a regular supply of water is very important. Sometimes, despite your best efforts to keep his dish full of cool, clean H_2O, your golden will seek refreshment from other available sources.*

Left: *Taking to the skies to snag an incoming Frisbee, this golden exhibits the athleticism and energy that, along with a warm temperament, are hallmarks of the breed.*

The owner of these two goldens likely gave up attempts to keep the dogs off the couch long ago—the sheepskin covering is an unmistakable sign that this is now golden territory.

Above: *With a log-sized chew toy freshly uncovered in a snowy backyard, a burly golden lounges seemingly unfazed by the cold, cold ground.*

Early Bird Memories

by Todd Tanner

 Todd Tanner has had golden retrievers in his life since he was a little boy. A Montana-based fly-fishing guide and outdoors writer, Tanner's writing has been published in *Field & Stream, Fly Fisherman, Retriever Journal,* and other hunting and fishing magazines.

In this story, Tanner writes with passion about his first experience with hunting. He is introduced to this new world by his father—and by Judy, a golden retriever with the hunt ingrained in her soul.

Todd Tanner's Judy was a golden retriever with the hunt ingrained in her soul.

At the end of a day in the field, a boy, his dad, and their golden prepare to load up and head home.

I WAS RAISED in a house where two things were paramount: honesty and golden retrievers. I occasionally, in moments of weakness, managed to slip sideways around the honesty thing—"Yes, Mom, my homework is done," or, "Believe me, Mrs. Grassi, my intentions toward your daughter are purely honorable"—but I never did get away from the golden retrievers. For the last 32 years, ever since my father brought Judy home to his wife and three children, there's been a golden in my life.

My father was a bird hunter, and the proudest moment of my young existence was when he decided that I was old enough to follow along on his hunts. I think I was eight; I didn't have a gun, and I didn't have brush pants to keep the thorns out of legs, and I wasn't allowed to do anything except stay directly behind my dad. It didn't matter—it was magic.

We hunted on a huge old abandoned farm that had been allowed to grow over. It was called Mt. Tom or Cow Hill depending on who you talked to, and it was on the other side of the big swamp behind our house. Judy, who was at once the ugliest dog in the world and also the best, would cast back and forth in front of my dad until she hit a fresh trail, and then would go hard and fast after the bird. Dad would turn to me and say, "See how she's working the scent? Look at her tail go." He always seemed to know what type of bird she was on, whether it was a pheasant or a woodcock or a grouse, and he'd declare, "She's on a rooster and it's running. Come on, we've got to keep up." Or "It's a woodcock. We can take our time." He was never wrong.

Judy knew all about hunting season, and she'd wait patiently for my father to say, "Okay, girl, let's go. Up in the truck." If it

Right: *Looking a tad serious despite the sunshine of a warm winter day, a golden with a luxuriant coat waits for a signal from its master.*

Below: *"The owner of a golden retriever is doubly blessed since he can have his cake and eat it too. For the Golden is not only gorgeous but is a good gun dog as well."*—David Michael Duffy, Outdoor Life, *June 1964*

turned out that my dad couldn't hunt for a few days, she'd hang around until it was late enough in the afternoon that there was no chance they'd get out, and then she'd sneak into the swamp behind the house. An hour or two later she'd be back, coated with mud and muck, and carrying a muskrat or a cock pheasant in her mouth. The pheasants were always dead, but she'd bring the muskrats home alive just to show us, and then she'd walk over and drop them near the brook by the side of the house. They'd scurry down to the edge of the stream, look back at Judy like they couldn't quite believe what had happened, then dive in and head back to wherever they lived. It wouldn't surprise me to find out that even now, 25 or 30 generations later, the muskrats in that swamp sit around at night and tell strange tales of a great, gangly, golden retriever with an amazingly soft mouth.

My father was always an excellent shot. I can remember standing behind him, amazed, as Judy flushed two cock pheasants from a dense thicket 25 yards away. He swung his Belgian-made Browning 12-gauge and fired twice in the single instant it took me to recognize what was happening. Both birds fell, feathers trailing them to the ground like autumn leaves, and Judy did double work, retrieving first one and then the other. I helped tuck the roosters in the back of my father's canvas game vest, fascinated with their colors and their feel and proud as an eight-year old boy could be that I was a part of the whole wondrous experience. Judy stood there, looking back and forth from my father to me and wagging her tail, as if saying to Dad, "It's about time you got the pup out in the field for some training. He belongs in the woods, not playing football in the backyard."

When we got back home, Dad cleaned the birds and then told me to take them outside and pluck them. I sat down under the old maple tree near our garage and pulled out little wisps of feathers that disappeared into the carpet of red and gold leaves at my feet. When I finished I looked at the two birds, now no different than the chickens my mother stuffed and cooked on Sunday nights, and wondered at the sadness I felt. I couldn't help but think that I'd taken things of beauty and somehow turned them ugly and ordinary. I didn't understand until years later that hunting and sorrow inevitably go hand in hand, that the sadness we feel when we kill is the keen edge that sharpens our appreciation for all life.

Dad's gone now, to cancer five years ago, and Judy died in '73, but that old canvas vest with the shell holders and the leather shoulder patch, the one Dad wore every time he went after birds with Judy and me, is still hanging in the closet at my folks' house. I noticed it the last time I was home to visit, hanging forgotten next to my Dad's red and black checkered wool hunting jacket. Even now, 27 years later, the sight of that vest can take me back in time to Mt. Tom, back to the brush and the roosters and the image of a tall, dark-haired man and a golden retriever who lived to hunt.

Above: *Three wet, muddy goldens sludge back to their owner with some impressive-looking logs.*
Left: *A hunter pauses to scratch the ruff of his beautiful golden.*

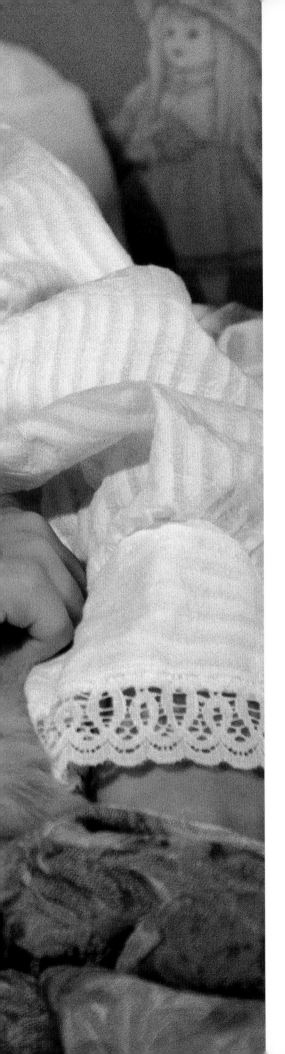

PART III

A Place in Our Hearts

"There are no more appealing and lovable pups in the world than the rotund, bear-cublike balls of fluffy yellow hair that are Golden retriever pups. Call it eye appeal, sex appeal, mother-instinct appeal or what have you, but the Golden has it."
David Michael Duffy, *Outdoor Life*, May 1968

Above: *A pile of puppies engage in a healthy wrestle.*
Left: *A golden retriever warms the heart of every member of the family. But it is arguably with children that the strongest bond forms.*

Broken Treaty

by Dion Henderson

 Once you let a golden retriever into your life, the dog will quickly find a permanent place in your heart. There's just something about that kind temperament and desire to please that gets you "right there." You don't need to know anything else about the dog—only that it's a golden retriever, and all will be fine.

Dion Henderson wrote from the heart of the Upper Midwest. He worked for the Associated Press's Wisconsin Bureau for more than forty years and held the position of bureau chief for fifteen years until his death in 1984. An author of eight books, including three novels, Henderson also wrote hundreds of articles for national magazines, including *Collier's*, *The Saturday Evening Post*, and *Field & Stream*.

The devotion of a golden to its master is remarkable; the bond between the two is strong as steel. Henderson tells the story of Golden Recollection, nicknamed Wreck, a very old retriever that stays devoted until his master lets him know it's time to go.

A working golden retriever in the field braves the elements of a late-autumn blanket of snow.

WE HAD WALKED down the beach and around the bay and finally out to where the point stabbed into the big lake to watch the ducks come home from the cornfields. While we were watching the ducks we saw Doc's old dog and watched him, too. He was old, incredibly old, more than a hundred years old as you reckon the age of a man, and he walked very carefully on the little stones as though he knew that everything inside him was very fragile and might break if he jarred any of it.

We watched him move down the steps, a big taffy-colored dog still very handsome, as some golden retrievers are, and at the bottom of the steps he did not hesitate at all, but turned after us, tracking easily on the beach. "Old, old," Doc said. "Golden Recollection. I hope I do not grow so old."

"Or if you do, that you grow old as beautifully as Wreck," I added.

"What's the difference?" Doc asked. "You get so terribly old, and then you are at the end of it."

I didn't say anything. Maybe it makes no difference how you get there. Maybe it does. The old dog was still tracking us, not wasting any motion, and down at the far end of the bay he stopped altogether. For a moment I thought he was resting, but he hadn't stopped for that. It was something the wind told him, and he had turned his head out toward the lake.

The ducks were coming in occasionally now, crossing us high up and heading for their rafts in open water, and the bay was rippling lightly in the breeze. Earlier the wind had been stronger from the bluffs, and now the water was flecked with floating oak leaves.

Abruptly the old dog gathered himself and slid into the water, still being very careful but clearly very determined too.

"Chasing a leaf," Doc said wearily. "And with his rheumatism. It'll take me an hour to rub some life back into him."

But it wasn't a leaf. You do not smell a leaf, and the old dog went into the water because the nose he had by rightful inheritance from Lord Tweedmouth's long-ago bloodhound told him to go. He swam very low in the water and so slowly that it sometimes seemed he did not move at all. Nearly a hundred yards out, a leaf that was not a leaf flapped a startled wing and quacked once in alarm as it was engulfed. The old dog then veered toward the nearest shore, which was very close to us. He took a long time, and you could hear him breathing all the way.

When he was in shallow water, he stopped and let the water support him until his breathing was even again. Then he came out and started casting for our trail again, and Doc called him.

Wreck came on, wavering a little, and sat down proudly with the crippled duck and held it until Doc said, "Thank you, sir," and put out his hand. The old dog put the bird there and stood up to shake, but he could not quite make it. He tried, looked up with a

Golden retrievers are second only to Labrador retrievers in their skill at fetching downed waterfowl. This golden swims back to the duck blind with a mallard drake firmly—but gently—gripped in its mouth.

A motley trio along the edge of a
Montana stream.

wry expression on his face as though it did not surprise him greatly,
and then lay down on the stones and suddenly was exhausted. I took
the duck, and Doc wrapped the big dog in his jacket and carried
him all the way home. "You see what I mean?" Doc said over his
shoulder. "What can you do with a dog like this?"

"I don't know," I replied, because I did not want any part of the
decision he was trying to make. "I don't know very much about
retrievers."

When the old kennel hands begin to talk of memorable dogs,
one of the things they remember best is the royal manner—the
flashing stride, the relentless courage, the flare of style and the

champion's heart. Such dogs do not always achieve royal standing in the world of dog competitions, because they do not always have the chance; but when they do, they know that they do, and they are as proud as a man of the achievement.

Golden Recollection won his bench championship on the main line when the majors were few and far between, and he had finished the campaigning with a sporting-group win. His field work was very distinguished too, although his best seasons were before the face-to-face competition of the National as it is today. He was aging during the time of the compiled championships, and I suppose you would say he was the dawn of the goldens' day that came in with Midas, who either won or did not win the first real National, and Nitro Express and the later great ones.

He wasn't Doc's dog, you understand. His registration was dated the year Doc had entered fourth grade, and this summer that they came to the lake shore together was the year Doc finished his internship. It did not seem possible that a dog's life could span such a time.

Most people have to accustom themselves to living through several generations of dogs. But in Wreck's case it was reversed, and he was well along in his second generation of people, because men don't live forever either.

So Doc and the dog who had been his father's contemporary were living in the same house again, but conditions were changed considerably from the time they had been the famous champion and the schoolboy, and naturally there were many complications. For one thing, Doc got married in the spring before he was quite ready to set up a practice, and he had quite a few problems that were strictly his own. His wife was very pretty and very brave, as any girl has to be who marries a young doctor, and she was very good about the dog, too.

But there is one thing about a handsome and polite dog you pet occasionally when you visit his home, and it is another thing entirely to have a heedless old monarch with all the weakness of that age and condition accept you as his handmaiden. I don't think she complained, then or later, about the obvious nuisance that Wreck was around the house. The first morning I met her, when she and Doc came to the old cottage from the city, I heard something special in the way she looked at the dog and said, "Poor old fellow."

There is a way a woman has of saying things like that; you can tell when you hear the sadness in her voice. She does not say exactly what she means, and maybe she does not even know exactly what she means; but you know, and a dog knows too, after a while. So I did not become involved any of the times that Doc asked, sort of casually, "What do you do with an old dog?" The time I came closest was the day after Wreck went for the duck. It was a cool morning, the dew not quite a frost but glistening very close to it on the shady side of the trees.

Doc and his wife were having breakfast on the porch and called me in for coffee. Wreck was lying where the morning sun streamed in on him, and once I heard him move and looked at him sharply. He was inching his way across the floor to keep fully in the sun, because that was how he had to move, with the chill and dampness of night heavy on the old bones. But he saw me watching him, and though he looked back at me did not invite help; so I let him alone. Two or three other times he moved the same way, but when I left an hour later the sun had soaked through the caramel-colored hide and the blood was moving and a warm dog is not nearly so old as a cold dog.

Outside, Doc explained, "It hurts his pride if you help him. What are you going to do with a dog like that?"

"It depends on you and it depends on the dog," I said. "And it depends on the association that has developed between you and the way each of you has accepted it and a number of other things that there is no point discussing."

"We've negotiated a treaty," Doc said. "The old guy is happy—I guess he's happy."

And I guess he was, in his way. He did not really feel very bad about being old. He moved carefully always, and on warm, dry afternoons when he had been in the sun quite a while he would play very sedately all by himself. Then he would draw a very clear line to the playing and look at you wryly, and you knew he was up against the boundary he had made for himself. It was a

A summer day at the lake has put this golden to contemplating a dive into the cool waters.

Five goldens wait for their owners to get the rest of the gear loaded in the truck so they can head for home.

little like being around a famous old athlete who occasionally worked out ever so little, in imitation of himself as a young man, then paused apologetically because he could not in modesty indicate just how beautifully and easily he had done the physical things that hardly anyone could do so well any more.

And plainly Golden Recollection did not think of himself as a nuisance, not to anybody. Sometimes when he was sleeping on the pier and the sun moved away from him behind the trees he could not move very well, but he was very patient and expected someone would come for him after a while. Someone always did, and might say, "Poor old dog," which made a strange, flat look come in his eyes as though he heard what I heard in the words.

"He earned a lot of things in his time," Doc said. "I guess he figures he earned enough to retire on."

Then it was getting to be time for Doc and his wife to move back to the city to a little apartment, and there got to be a feeling of strain around the cottage. Every time his wife looked at Wreck she looked as though she might cry, and one time Doc told her: "You couldn't take a dog who's been a house dog all that length of time and put him in a boarding kennel. You might as well kill him outright."

When he said that, his wife did start to cry, and I thought it was a pretty good time for me not to be around any more. Doc walked out with me, and we headed along the shore toward my place, but he did not say anything, and neither did I. Opposite the point we stopped for a while and watched the big mergansers working in the bay. Presently there was a rushing in the leaves behind us, and there was Wreck, walking very carefully, but coming on just the same.

"Fifteen years ago," Doc said, sounding partly proud and partly exasperated, "my father told Wreck to look after me, and he's still doing it. When I was a kid and wanted to go fishing in the canoe by myself, he used to make me take Wreck with me, and he'd say, 'Look after the kid, Wreck.' And all the time we were fishing, the dog would lie there in the canoe and watch me."

"I remember. He pulled you out once, didn't he?"

"He sure did." Doc grinned a little. "It was in four feet of water, but it was swimming depth for him, so he pulled me out. Pretty near broke my arm in the process, but Dad thought it was fine."

The dog reached us by then and sat down next to Doc and looked at him briefly with those old, old eyes.

"That's the same expression." Doc was almost angry. "He doesn't really give a damn about me. But the old man said he should look out for me, and he'll do it if he has to live thirty years more."

I guess that pretty well stated the case. Wreck did not really love anyone any more; he had outlived all his young loves, but he still had a job to do, and he did not propose to quit. You never know what goes on in a dog's head. He will do a thing, and there are various

Facing page: *Reeling in a rainbow trout at sunrise, a fisherman chooses to share the experience with his best friend.*

A golden retriever returns with a ring-necked pheasant.

ways to explain it. The best way usually is the simple and instinctive way, but I am not sure it is always right. In the end, there is really no way to tell.

The next day I went past Doc's cottage in a boat, well out, but I could see they were taking down screens and putting boxes in the car. I wondered about the dog. It was automatic to think of him at that point, and soon I saw the golden heap lying in the sun in sight of everything or at least in range of ear and nose. When you have

dogs for a long time and keep them for the quality they have that is quite beyond compromise, you make many treaties that are hard to keep.

I thought about the dogs and the treaties, and I was grateful for the dog in the boat with me. She was one of the German dogs who was far from home and who, knowing she would never see home again, looked at the world with ice-cold eyes. She did her work marvelously and she gave me puppies who would love passionately and cling hard to life, but she did not offer anything like that and she wouldn't accept it, and I was grateful for her.

But however they are, you do whatever you have to do, and I expected that Doc and his wife would take the old dog with them. Long after dark, the two of them came to my door.

"Wreck's gone," Doc blurted out. "We've been looking for hours."

"My boots are in the closet," I said. "Just a minute. What happened?"

"He followed Doc out in the field." His wife had been crying again. "Then he started to come back by himself and got lost."

I stopped putting on my boots. There was an expression on Doc's face.

"All right. What happened?" I asked.

"He left me," Doc's voice was a little hoarse. "The gun misfired, and he looked at me and left me."

"No," his wife said. "You didn't!"

"It seemed like the best thing to do," Doc said. "I didn't plan it. I could have given him an intravenous a lot more easily. But then he'd have known. The way it was, I heard crows tormenting something up in the field, and I took the gun and went back to see what it was. I was away back there watching them, and Wreck came along trailing me. It wasn't a good day for him, and he had a lot of trouble walking. Once he fell down, and I was afraid he couldn't get up again; but he did. He got up to me, breathing very hard and pretty shaky, but he gave me that quick glance then went on out into the field to see what the crows were doing." Doc was sweating now.

"All of a sudden I thought, 'Here it is. No fuss, and it won't hurt him at all.' And I brought up the gun and pulled the trigger." He wiped his face like a kid, and the sweat followed right after it. "It misfired," he said. "It never did that before. And there he was, looking at me right down the barrel, with the little gold bead right on his head. I put the gun down, and I knew that I couldn't ever do it again and that we'd keep him as long as he was happy. And I called him to come."

"But he didn't come," I prompted.

"No," Doc said. "He looked at me in a way that he'd never looked before, sort of relieved, and took a big breath and walked away from me better than he's walked for months."

"And you thought he was going home?"

"No," Doc said. "I knew he wasn't going home. I knew it, all right."

There was not much else for anyone to say, and there really wasn't any need to look for him that night. In the morning we went out to the field and lined ourselves up with the place that had been home to Wreck for so long then suddenly was not home any more, and we walked in a straight line away from it. After a while we came to the water's edge, and there was all that remained of Golden Recollection.

"I wonder what happened," said Doc's wife.

"He did not need to live any more," I told her. "Your husband knows what that means."

"Yes," Doc said. "Now I do."

Left: *Bounding with energy a mom plays with her posse of pups.*
Below: *Golden retriever siblings on a winter day.*

Brutus and Me

by John J. Kelley

"All right, my friend, let's go . . ."

My oldest running partner turns 8 today.

I use "oldest" in two senses: First, in loyalty, stick-to-it-iveness, whatever, this ol' buddy has "stayed the course" longer than any other running partner. The second is chronological. If the accepted computation is correct, Brutus's 8 dog years equal 56 of the human kind.

When attempting to compose a birthday tribute for Brutus, I tend to think of the utterances of the great naturalist-philosopher Henry David Thoreau. Probably because, like Thoreau, my canine sidekick and I have spent so much of our companionate traveling time on trails.

One phrase in particular springs to mind. It sums up the elusive quarry Brutus and I pursue out there: "I long ago lost a hound, a bay horse and a turtledove, and am still on their trail."

Like all runners, Brutus and I are romantic questers, captivated not by the capture but the chase. And that is what inspires in both of us the same tail thumping excitement as we set out, day after day, over paths so familiar we could run them by night as well as by day.

Except in the hottest weather, our enthusiasm remains unspent at the finish of our usual 7- to 12-mile trek. Given a recuperative splash in the Thames River and a couple of minutes to shake out the water, Brutus hankers for a second round.

But, liberated as we appear in the course of our prancing, we both belong to the human rat race and seldom, if ever, have time left for second helpings. So the old boy obediently settles down to await tomorrow's excursion, and to dream, perhaps, of bay horses and turtledoves.

Somewhere in *Walden,* Thoreau addresses the recurrent question as to why he preferred his hermit's solitude to human society. He calls the custom of family dining "giving each other a taste of the same old musty cheese that we are." Sad as the observation seems, it also seems sadly true that human beings do tire of each other.

To his great credit, Brutus has never shown the teeniest sign of tiring of me.

Now I tell you straight that I frequently tire of my own musty cheese thoughts. I am cursed by a constitutional moodiness, assailed by demons of depression. Some days find me lifting a thousand pounds, psychologically speaking, with each step.

On such days few, if any, humans could abide my company. On such days, left to myself, I probably wouldn't undertake a run, preferring instead to curl up in the fetal position, lost in Hamlet-style musings.

Today is one of those days. I'm hunkering down in a kind of sitting fetal position, behind my trusty typewriter, planning nothing more physical than a retreat into the "Walden" or the "Hamlet" of my mind.

Only there kerplunks ol' Brutus between my feet, his irresistible golden retriever eyes imploring us out.

"Hey, how about it, my friend?" he seems to be saying. "Things aren't really that bad, you'll see, once we start running. Come on, let's do it. Let's blow out those cobwebs."

And all of a sudden I realize it's his birthday. And all he wants is to lift me out of the kitchen, out of my glooms and onto the trails, green with summer.

"All right, my friend, let's go," I say.

He needs no second call.

As the door clicks behind us, I feel the cobwebs dissipating. For all we know, there's a bay horse out there waiting to be run down.

John J. Kelley, the 1957 Boston Marathon champion and a two-time Olympic marathoner, is the running columnist for the New London (Conn.) Day.

It's not the wisest thing in the world to leave a strawberry milkshake—complete with whipped topping and a cherry—unattended with a golden retriever in the vicinity.

Above: *Barely able to get a bite on a tennis ball that is bigger than its snout, a golden retriever puppy plays around in a pool that is just the right size.*
Left: *A boat is an intriguing locale to explore, and these three golden pups peek their eyes above the gunwales for just a moment before being distracted by some previously unexplored facet of this fiberglass world.*

Above: *Goldens are efficient retrievers and most will take to water from a very early age.*
Left: *A log is not too much to handle for this golden intent on bringing a "gift" to its master.*

Above: *Hunters with goldens enjoy many wonderful days afield.*
Facing page: *"Every time I hunt with a golden there's an urge to croon 'Moon River,' eat Philadelphia cream cheese, and snuggle under chamois sheets. The dogs are that simpatico, that laid back. But don't let that pliability mislead you. Sturdy of mind and hard of frame, they are. Fit companions for the long haul, from the rugged pleasures of the bird field to the silent lives shared in the same dirt through eternity."*—Bill Tarrant, Gun Dog Training: New Strategies from Today's Top Trainers, *1996*
Overleaf: *Four surprisingly mellow puppies observe the backyard goings-on from the stoop.*

Mrs. Donovan

by James Herriot

 The late veterinarian and author James Herriot did not write his first book until he was into his fifth decade, but since the publication of *All Creatures Great and Small* in the 1970s, his wonderful essays on his many years in veterinary practice and his stories for children have made him one of the most cherished writers of the twentieth century. Scottish by birth, Herriot practiced veterinary medicine in Yorkshire, England, where he wrote many of his books, including *All Things Bright and Beautiful, All Things Wise and Wonderful, The Lord God Made Them All, Every Living Thing,* and *James Herriot's Yorkshire.* His books for children include *Moses the Kitten, Only One Woof,* and *The Market Square Dog,* among numerous others. Herriot always portrayed the animals he wrote about in a humane and loving voice.

This is the story of Mrs. Donovan, a dog-lover with a kind heart, and the story of Roy, a classic golden looking for a new start in life.

A fluffy golden pup.

A girl poses for a family portrait with her four-pack of golden puppies.

THE SILVERY-HAIRED OLD gentleman with the pleasant face didn't look the type to be easily upset but his eyes glared at me angrily and his lips quivered with indignation.

"Mr. Herriot," he said, "I have come to make a complaint. I strongly object to your callousness in subjecting my dog to unnecessary suffering."

"Suffering? What suffering?" I was mystified.

"I think you know, Mr. Herriot. I brought my dog in a few days ago. He was very lame and I am referring to your treatment on that occasion."

I nodded. "Yes, I remember it well. . . but where does the suffering come in?"

"Well, the poor animal is going around with his leg dangling and I have it on good authority that the bone is fractured and should have been put in plaster immediately." The old gentleman stuck his chin out fiercely.

"All right, you can stop worrying," I said. "Your dog has a radial paralysis caused by a blow on the ribs and if you are patient and follow my treatment he'll gradually improve. In fact I think he'll recover completely."

"But he trails his leg when he walks."

"I know—that's typical, and to the layman it does give the appearance of a broken leg. But he shows no sign of pain, does he?"

"No, he seems quite happy, but this lady seemed to be absolutely sure of her facts. She was adamant."

"Lady?"

"Yes," said the old gentleman. "She is clever with animals and she came round to see if she could help in my dog's convalescence. She brought some excellent condition powders with her."

"Ah!" A blinding shaft pierced the fog in my mind. All was suddenly clear. "It was Mrs. Donovan, wasn't it?"

"Well . . . er, yes. That was her name."

Old Mrs. Donovan was a woman who really got around. No matter what was going on in Darrowby—weddings, funerals, house-sales—you'd find the dumpy little figure and walnut face among the spectators, the darting, black-button eyes taking everything in. And always, on the end of its lead, her terrier dog.

When I say "old," I'm only guessing, because she appeared ageless; she seemed to have been around a long time but she could have been anything between fifty-five and seventy-five. She certainly had the vitality of a young woman because she must have walked vast distances in her dedicated quest to keep abreast of events. Many people took an uncharitable view of her acute curiosity but whatever the motivation, her activities took her into almost every channel of life in the town. One of these channels was our veterinary practice.

Because Mrs. Donovan, among her other widely ranging

interests, was an animal doctor. In fact I think it would be safe to say that this facet of her life transcended all the others.

She could talk at length on the ailments of small animals and she had a whole armoury of medicines and remedies at her command, her two specialties being her miracle working condition powders and a dog shampoo of unprecedented value for improving the coat. She had an uncanny ability to sniff out a sick animal, and it was not uncommon when I was on my rounds to find Mrs. Donovan's dark gipsy face poised intently over what I had thought was my patient while she administered calf's foot jelly or one of her own patent nostrums.

I suffered more than Siegfried because I took a more active part in the small animal side of our practice. I was anxious to develop this aspect and to improve my image in this field and Mrs. Donovan didn't help at all. "Young Mr. Herriot," she would confide to my clients, "is all right with cattle and such like, but he don't know nothing about dogs and cats."

And of course they believed her and had implicit faith in her. She had the irresistible mystic appeal of the amateur and on top of that there was her habit, particularly endearing in Darrowby, of never charging for her advice, her medicines, her long periods of diligent nursing.

Older folk in the town told how her husband, an Irish farm worker, had died many years ago and how he must have had a "bit put away" because Mrs. Donovan had apparently been able to indulge all her interests over the years without financial strain. Since she inhabited the streets of Darrowby all day and every day I often encountered her and she always smiled up at me sweetly and told me how she had been sitting up all night with Mrs. So-and-so's dog that I'd been treating. She felt sure she'd be able to pull it through.

There was no smile on her face, however, on the day when she rushed into the surgery while Siegfried and I were having tea.

"Mr. Herriot!" she gasped. "Can you come? My little dog's been run over!"

I jumped up and ran out to the car with her. She sat in the passenger seat with her head bowed, her hands clasped tightly on her knees.

"He slipped his collar and ran in front of a car," she murmured. "He's lying in front of the school half-way up Cliffend Road. Please hurry."

I was there within three minutes but as I bent over the dusty little body stretched on the pavement I knew there was nothing I could do. The fast-glazing eyes, the faint, gasping respirations, the ghastly pallor of the mucous membranes all told the same story.

"I'll take him back to the surgery and get some saline into him, Mrs. Donovan," I said. "But I'm afraid he's had a massive internal haemorrhage. Did you see what happened exactly?"

She gulped. "Yes, the wheel went right over him."

Ruptured liver, for sure. I passed my hands under the little animal and began to lift him gently, but as I did so the breathing stopped and the eyes stared fixedly ahead.

Mrs. Donovan sank to her knees and for a few moments she gently stroked the rough hair of the head and chest. "He's dead, isn't he?" she whispered at last.

"I'm afraid he is," I said.

She got slowly to her feet and stood bewilderedly among the little group of bystanders on the pavement. Her lips moved but she seemed unable to say any more.

I took her arm, led her over to the car and opened the door. "Get in and sit down," I said. "I'll run you home. Leave everything to me."

I wrapped the dog in my calving overall and laid him in the boot before driving away. It wasn't until we drew up outside Mrs. Donovan's house that she began to weep silently. I sat there without speaking till she had finished. Then she wiped her eyes and turned to me.

"Do you think he suffered at all?"

"I'm certain he didn't. It was all so quick—he wouldn't know a thing about it."

With such an overwhelming desire to please and a need to connect with all things human, a golden will sometimes maneuver itself within range of some aggressive petting, regardless of whether that is what its owner had in mind.

She tried to smile. "Poor little Rex, I don't know what I'm going to do without him. We've travelled a few miles together, you know."

"Yes, you have. He had a wonderful life, Mrs. Donovan. And let me give you a bit of advice—you must get another dog. You'd be lost without one."

She shook her head. "No, I couldn't. That little dog meant too much to me. I couldn't let another take his place."

"Well I know that's how you feel just now but I wish you'd think about it. I don't want to seem callous—I tell everybody this when they lose an animal and I know it's good advice."

"Mr. Herriot, I'll never have another one." She shook her head again, very decisively. "Rex was my faithful friend for many years and I just want to remember him. He's the last dog I'll ever have."

I often saw Mrs. Donovan around the town after this and I was glad to see she was still as active as ever, though she looked strangely incomplete without the little dog on its lead. But it must have been

Golden retrievers are athletic and will pretty much hold your pace under any conditions.

over a month before I had the chance to speak to her.

It was on the afternoon that Inspector Halliday of the RSPCA rang me.

"Mr. Herriot," he said, "I'd like you to come and see an animal with me. A cruelty case."

"Right, what is it?"

"A dog, and it's pretty grim. A dreadful case of neglect." He gave me the name of a row of old brick cottages down by the river and said he'd meet me there.

Halliday was waiting for me, smart and business-like in his dark uniform, as I pulled up in the back lane behind the houses. He was a big, blond man with cheerful blue eyes but he didn't smile as he came over to the car.

"He's in here," he said, and led the way towards one of the doors in the long, crumbling wall. A few curious people were hanging around and with a feeling of inevitability I recognized a gnome-like brown face. Trust Mrs. Donovan, I thought, to be among those present at a time like this.

We went through the door into the long garden. I had found that even the lowliest dwellings in Darrowby had long strips of land at the back as though the builders had taken it for granted that the country people who were going to live in them would want to occupy themselves with the pursuits of the soil; with vegetable and fruit growing, even stock keeping in a small way. You usually found a pig there, a few hens, often pretty beds of flowers.

But this garden was a wilderness. A chilling air of desolation hung over the few gnarled apple and plum trees standing among a tangle of rank grass as though

the place had been forsaken by all living creatures.

Halliday went over to a ramshackle wooden shed with peeling paint and a rusted corrugated iron roof. He produced a key, unlocked the padlock and dragged the door partly open. There was no window and it wasn't easy to identify the jumble inside: broken gardening tools, an ancient mangle, rows of flower pots and partly used paint tins. And right at the back, a dog sitting quietly.

I didn't notice him immediately because of the gloom and because the smell in the shed started me coughing, but as I drew closer I saw that he was a big animal, sitting very upright, his collar secured by a chain to a ring in the wall. I had seen some thin dogs but this advanced emaciation reminded me of my text books on anatomy; nowhere else did the bones of pelvis, face and rib cage stand out with such horrifying clarity. A deep, smoothed-out hollow in the earth floor showed where he had lain, moved about, in fact lived for a very long time.

The sight of the animal had a stupefying effect on me; I only half took in the rest of the scene—the filthy shreds of sacking scattered nearby, the bowl of scummy water.

"Look at his back end," Halliday muttered.

I carefully raised the dog from his sitting position and realised that the stench in the place was not entirely due to the piles of excrement. The hindquarters were a welter of pressure sores which had turned gangrenous, and strips of sloughing tissue hung down from them. There were similar sores along the sternum and ribs. The coat, which seemed to be a dull yellow, was matted and caked with dirt.

The Inspector spoke again. "I don't think he's ever been out of here. He's only a young dog—about a year old—but I understand he's been in this shed since he was an eight-week-old pup. Somebody out in the lane heard a whimper or he'd never have been found."

I felt a tightening of the throat and a sudden nausea which wasn't due to the smell. It was the thought of this patient animal sitting starved and forgotten in the darkness and filth for a year. I looked again at the dog and saw in his eyes only a calm trust. Some dogs would have barked their heads off and soon been discovered, some would have become terrified and vicious, but this was one of the totally undemanding kind, the kind which had complete faith in people and accepted all their actions without complaint. Just an occasional whimper perhaps as he sat interminably in the empty blackness which had been his world and at times wondered what it was all about.

"Well, Inspector, I hope you're going to throw the book at whoever's responsible," I said.

Halliday grunted. "Oh, there won't be much done. It's a case of diminished responsibility. The owner's definitely simple. Lives with

Facing page: *"The golden retriever is certainly blessed with beauty."* —*Joe Stetson,* Field & Stream, *December 1963*

an aged mother who hardly knows what's going on either. I've seen the fellow and it seems he threw in a bit of food when he felt like it and that's about all he did. They'll fine him and stop him keeping an animal in the future but nothing more than that."

"I see." I reached out and stroked the dog's head and he immediately responded by resting a paw on my wrist. There was a pathetic dignity about the way he held himself erect, the calm eyes regarding me, friendly and unafraid. "Well, you'll let me know if you want me in court."

"Of course, and thank you for coming along." Halliday hesitated for a moment. "And now I expect you'll want to put this poor thing out of his misery right away."

I continued to run my hand over the head and ears while I thought for a moment. "Yes . . . yes, I suppose so. We'd never find a home for him in this state. It's the kindest thing to do. Anyway, push the door wide open will you so that I can get a proper look at him."

In the improved light I examined him more thoroughly. Perfect teeth, well-proportioned limbs with a fringe of yellow hair. I put my stethoscope on his chest and as I listened to the slow, strong thudding of the heart the dog again put his paw on my hand.

I turned to Halliday. "You know, Inspector, inside this bag of bones there's a lovely healthy Golden Retriever. I wish there was some way of letting him out."

As I spoke I noticed there was more than one figure in the door opening. A pair of black pebble eyes were peering intently at the big dog from behind the Inspector's broad back. The other spectators had remained in the lane but Mrs. Donovan's curiosity had been too much for her. I continued conversationally as though I hadn't seen her.

"You know, what this dog needs first of all is a good shampoo to clean up his matted coat."

"Huh?" said Halliday.

"Yes. And then he wants a long course of some really strong condition powders."

"What's that?" The Inspector looked startled.

"There's no doubt about it," I said. "It's the only hope for him, but where are you going to find such things? Really powerful enough, I mean." I sighed and straightened up. "Ah well, I suppose there's nothing else for it. I'd better put him to sleep right away. I'll get the things from my car."

With a "just-get-it-over-with" look, a golden puppy gets a thorough scrub down in the kitchen sink.

When I got back to the shed Mrs. Donovan was already inside examining the dog despite the feeble remonstrances of the big man.

"Look!" she said excitedly, pointing to a name roughly scratched on the collar. "His name's Roy." She smiled up at me. "It's a bit like Rex, isn't it, that name?"

"You know, Mrs. Donovan, now you mention it, it is. It's very like Rex, the way it comes off your tongue." I nodded seriously.

She stood silent for a few moments, obviously in the grip of a deep emotion, then she burst out.

"Can I have 'im? I can make him better, I know I can. Please, please let me have 'im!"

"Well I don't know," I said. "It's really up to the Inspector. You'll have to get his permission."

Halliday looked at her in bewilderment, then he said: "Excuse me, Madam," and drew me to one side. We walked a few yards through the long grass and stopped under a tree.

"Mr. Herriot," he whispered, "I don't know what's going on here, but I can't just pass over an animal in this condition to anybody who has a casual whim. The poor beggar's had one bad break already—I think it's enough. This woman doesn't look a suitable person . . ."

After its bath, the pup is toweled off by the youngster's owner to restore a more typical fluffball look, while the pup's sibling and mom swarm around the owner's feet.

I held up a hand. "Believe me, Inspector, you've nothing to worry about. She's a funny old stick but she's been sent from heaven today. If anybody in Darrowby can give this dog a new life it's her."

Halliday still looked very doubtful. "But I still don't get it. What was all that stuff about him needing shampoos and condition powders?"

"Oh never mind about that. I'll tell you some other time. What he needs is lots of good grub, care and affection, and that's just what he'll get. You can take my word for it."

"All right, you seem very sure." Halliday looked at me for a second or two then turned and walked over to the eager little figure by the shed.

❧ ❧ ❧

I had never before been deliberately on the lookout for Mrs. Donovan: she had just cropped up wherever I happened to be, but now I scanned the streets of Darrowby anxiously day by day without sighting her. I didn't like it when Gobber Newhouse got drunk and drove his bicycle determinedly through a barrier into a ten-foot hole where they were laying the new sewer and Mrs. Donovan was not in evidence among the happy crowd who watched the council workmen and

The American Kennel Club Standard of the Golden Retriever: A symmetrical, powerful, active dog, sound and well put together, not clumsy or long in leg, displaying a kindly expression and possessing a personality that is eager, alert and self-confident.

two policemen trying to get him out; and when she was nowhere to be seen when they had to fetch the fire engine to the fish and chip shop the night the fat burst into flames I became seriously worried.

Maybe I should have called round to see how she was getting on with that dog. Certainly I had trimmed off the necrotic tissue and dressed the sores before she took him away, but perhaps he needed something more than that. And yet at the time I had felt a strong conviction that the main thing was to get him out of there and clean him and feed him and nature would do the rest. And I had a lot of faith in Mrs. Donovan—far more than she had in me—when it came to animal doctoring; it was hard to believe I'd been completely wrong.

It must have been nearly three weeks and I was on the point of calling at her home when I noticed her stumping briskly along the far side of the market-place, peering closely into every shop window exactly as before. The only difference was that she had a big yellow dog on the end of the lead.

I turned the wheel and sent my car bumping over the cobbles till I was abreast of her. When she saw me getting out she stopped and smiled impishly, but she didn't speak as I bent over Roy and examined him. He was still a skinny dog but he looked bright and happy, his wounds were healthy and granulating and there was not a speck of dirt in his coat or on his skin. I knew then what Mrs. Donovan had been doing all this time; she had been washing and combing and teasing at that filthy tangle till she had finally conquered it.

As I straightened up she seized my wrist in a grip of surprising strength and looked up into my eyes.

"Now Mr. Herriot," she said, "haven't I made a difference to this dog!"

"You've done wonders, Mrs. Donovan," I said. "And you've been at him with that marvellous shampoo of yours, haven't you?"

She giggled and walked away and from that day I saw the two of them frequently but at a distance and something like two months went by before I had a chance to talk to her again. She was passing by the surgery as I was coming down the steps and again she grabbed my wrist.

"Mr. Herriot," she said, just as she had done before, "haven't

Golden retriever puppies, like kids everywhere, like to play. Mom encourages her youngster, keeping a loosely gripped tennis ball within reach.

Anybody for a game of Frisbee?

I made a difference to this dog!"

I looked down at Roy with something akin to awe. He had grown and filled out and his coat, no longer yellow but a rich gold, lay in luxuriant shining swathes over the well-fleshed ribs and back. A new, brightly studded collar glittered on his neck and his tail, beautifully fringed, fanned the air gently. He was now a Golden Retriever in full magnificence. As I stared at him he reared up, plunked his fore paws on my chest and looked into my face, and in his eyes I read plainly the same calm affection and trust I had seen back in that black, noisome shed.

"Mrs. Donovan," I said softly, "he's the most beautiful dog in Yorkshire." Then, because I knew she was waiting for it, "It's those wonderful condition powders. Whatever do you put in them?"

"Ah, wouldn't you like to know!" She bridled and smiled up at me coquettishly and indeed she was nearer being kissed at that moment than for many years.

☙ ☙ ☙

I suppose you could say that that was the start of Roy's second life. And as the years passed I often pondered on the beneficent providence which had decreed that an animal which had spent his first twelve months abandoned and unwanted, staring uncomprehendingly into that unchanging, stinking darkness, should be whisked in a moment into an existence of light and movement and love. Because I don't think any dog had it quite so good as Roy from then on.

His diet changed dramatically from odd bread crusts to best stewing steak and biscuit, meaty bones and a bowl of warm milk every evening. And he never missed a thing. Garden fetes, school sports, evictions, gymkhanas—he'd be there. I was pleased to note that as time went on Mrs. Donovan seemed to be clocking up an even greater daily mileage. Her expenditure on shoe leather must have been phenomenal, but of course it was absolute pie for Roy—a busy round in the morning, home for a meal, then straight out again; it was all go.

Mrs. Donovan didn't confine her activities to the town centre; there was a big stretch of common land down by the river where there were seats and people used to take their dogs for a gallop, and

Two particularly lenient owners enjoy coffee at the table with their dog-chow-chomping golden retriever.

she liked to get down there fairly regularly to check on the latest developments on the domestic scene. I often saw Roy loping majestically over the grass among a pack of assorted canines, and when he wasn't doing that he was submitting to being stroked or patted or generally fussed over. He was handsome and he just liked people; it made him irresistible.

It was common knowledge that his mistress had bought a whole selection of brushes and combs of various sizes with which she laboured over his coat. Some people said she had a little brush for his teeth, too, and it might have been true, but he certainly wouldn't need his nails clipped—his life on the roads would keep them down.

Mrs. Donovan, too, had her reward; she had a faithful companion by her side every hour of the day and night. But there was more to it than that; she had always had the compulsion to help and heal animals and the salvation of Roy was the high point of her life—a blazing triumph which never dimmed.

I know the memory of it was always fresh because many years later I was sitting on the sidelines at a cricket match and I saw the two of them; the old lady glancing keenly around her, Roy gazing placidly out at the field of play, apparently enjoying every ball. At the end of the match I watched them move away with the dispersing crowd; Roy would have been about twelve then and heaven only knows how old Mrs. Donovan must have been, but the big golden animal was trotting along effortlessly and his mistress, a little more bent perhaps and her head rather nearer the ground, was going very well.

When she saw me she came over and I felt the familiar tight grip on my wrist.

"Mr. Herriot," she said, and in the dark probing eyes the pride was still as warm, the triumph still as bursting new as if it had all happened yesterday.

"Mr. Herriot, haven't I made a difference to this dog!"

Golden retrievers are wonderful with children—and everyone else. This five year old shares a bath with a golden retriever friend.

An Exception to the Rule

by Doug Grow

❧

A golden retriever service dog. "Golden retrievers love offering someone a helpful paw, even if it entails a distressing moment for themselves. They are unselfish and unrestrained in their love and companionship and their offering of guidance."—Gerald and Loretta Hausman, The Mythology of Dogs, *1997*

Sometimes you've got to make exceptions.

So when Doug Olson, radiation oncologist at Fairview Southdale Hospital in Edina [Minnesota], heard about Mel, he weighed the potential negatives against the special circumstances, shrugged his shoulders and said, "Why not?"

And so it is that Mel, an 8-year-old golden retriever, is entering a third week of radiation treatment for cancer at Fairview Southdale, which, with one tail-wagging exception, is a hospital for people.

The physician made the exception because Mel is the eyes of Shelli Nicoson, who at age 32 is approaching legendary status at Fairview Southdale. Nicoson's a registered nurse who has been blind since 1988, a side effect of diabetes. She's a near-legend because not only did she refuse to allow blindness to drive her from nursing, but she refused to let misfortune drive the smile from her face.

Daily, Nicoson and Mel come to the hospital and do their work. She runs an after-care program for cardiac patients. Mel leads her on her forays through the maze of hospital hallways.

"We were a package deal," Nicoson said, laughing. "Everybody at the hospital wanted Mel and I said, 'the only way you get Mel is if you take me, too.'"

About a month ago, Nicoson noticed a marble-sized growth on Mel's right front paw. She took the dog to vets at the University of Minnesota, who diagnosed the tumor as cancerous and removed it.

Radiation therapy at the university was to follow the surgery, but the therapy presented a huge logistics problem for Nicoson. Because she relies on Metro Mobility for transportation, she would have lost a half-day's work for each of the three weeks of treatment Mel needed.

"I have learned that when you face problems in life, there are always options," Nicoson said. She considered her options and went to hospital administrators and asked if it would be possible to have the dog's radiation treatment done at Fairview Southdale.

Administrators said they would take the question to Minneapolis Radiation Oncology PA, the private company that runs radiation services at Fairview Southdale.

"There were some concerns," said Olson. "My biggest concern is the perception of the patients—that we're using a facility used for humans to treat a dog. I want people to understand that we're taking special precautions to clean the room after treatment. . . .

"The other major concern I had was that at a time when costs are so much a part of talk about medicine that we'd have people saying, 'Look, the dog's getting better care than me.' But this is a very special situation."

Olson not only agreed to do the work, but he's doing it for free.

The doctor, who owns two springer spaniels, has been amazed at how cooperative a patient Mel's been.

"The dog's been incredible," Olson said. "When we started this, I said, 'No way he'll sit still [for the radiation treatment].' But Shelli said he would, and by gosh, he's been motionless."

The key is that Nicoson's is the last voice Mel hears before everyone leaves the room where the radiation treatment occurs.

"What was happening at first," said Nicoson, "is that I'd say, 'Rest!' and Mel would lie perfectly still, but then, as we'd be leaving the room, someone would say something like, 'OK, Mel, good boy.' Mel would hear his name and of course lift his head, 'Somebody call me?' So we've learned that after I say, 'Rest!' everybody must leave quietly."

Under advice from the vets who are consulting with Olson, the dog receives much higher radiation dosages than human patients would receive. There are other differences in treating a working dog than in treating a human patient, Olson has learned. "I was talking to the vet today," said Olson, "and she's concerned about Mel becoming lame. She said, 'Look, this is a working dog; it would be better that he die of cancer than end up lame.' That means that I have to look at this differently than I would a human. With a human, we'd be more aggressive about treating the cancer, even if it meant having to cut off the foot." Nicoson, by the way, doesn't necessarily agree with the vet. If Mel ends up lame, she said, "He'll become my pet, my couch dog. I don't want anything to happen to Mel."

These are stressful times for Nicoson, for the thought of losing Mel, her eyes, partner and friend since 1988, is overwhelming. "Mel gives me confidence, mobility and independence," Nicoson said. "Put those things together and they total life."

Because Mel is tender in the area of treatment, Olson decided to give him the day off from radiation Monday, a decision the dog greeted with a wag of his tail. Then, limping slightly, Mel did his work, leading Nicoson back to her work.

Doug Grow is a staff writer for the Minneapolis Star-Tribune.

A golden retriever and its eight-year-old owner lounge away the day on the living-room floor.

Two goldens sitting in a field of leaf balsam root flowers.

Below: *A golden was bred to retrieve, and he will do just that, bringing back ducks and grouse while hunting in the field or retrieving the evening paper on a summer day in the suburbs. Often, the golden will fetch whatever is fetchable—mittens, a backpack, a misplaced tube of toothpaste, or a carelessly tossed aside pair of underwear.*

Above: *Probably not quite getting the gist of the program it's watching, this golden nonetheless picks up on the fascination of its seven-year-old master and feigns interest—always within easy reach for some aggressive petting.*
Right: *The golden retriever has it all: spectacular beauty and a personality that will grab the heart of even the grumpiest grump.*
Overleaf: *One of these four pups scored the prime napping position by the food bowl should their owner decide it's suppertime.*

Left: *A young golden bounds over a snowy hill with a firm grip on a training dummy. Professional gun dog trainers advise that you never encourage your golden retriever, intended for hunting use, to retrieve anything but its training dummy. Retrieving a wide variety of items only confuses the dog when later hunting afield, and it may return with something other than the bird you just downed.*

Below: *Kind and cute, golden retrievers garner a lot of love from their owners. But ever unselfish, they shower an exponential amount of love right back.*

Despite the sunshine, this boy and his golden choose to stay behind closed doors.

A mother and her six-day-old puppies relax in their corner of the kitchen.

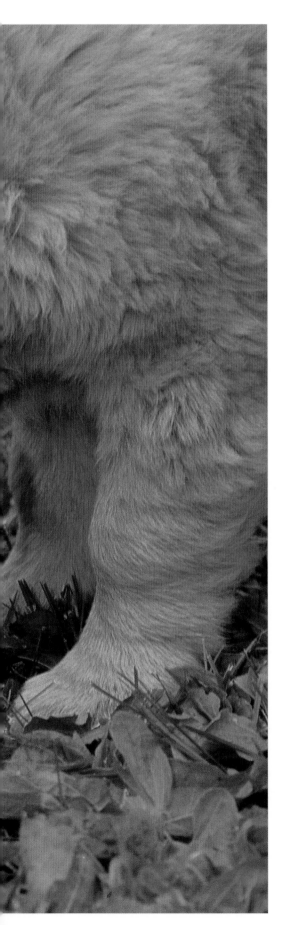

Above: *Many golden retriever trainers advise that you start training when your dog is quite young. Undoubtedly, a pup with this kind of initiative would be a star pupil.*

Left: *A bowl of water is just big enough for two pudgy snouts.*

About the Editor and Photographers

Todd R. Berger, a lifetime dog lover who has shared his life with too many dogs to count, is the editor of *Love of Labs* and two other anthologies on outdoors subjects. He is the acquisitions editor for Voyageur Press and a freelance writer based in St. Paul, Minnesota.
Photo © Tim Berger

Alan and Sandy Carey are freelance photographers based in Montana. Their images of the natural world and of dogs have been published in *National Geographic, Life, Audubon, Natural History, Readers Digest, Newsweek, Smithsonian, Ranger Rick, Time,* and numerous other magazines. Their work has also been published in several books, including *Love of Labs, Puppy Love, and Gun Dogs (Master Training Series),* all published by Voyageur Press.